ROUTLEDGE LIBRARY EDITIONS: LIBRARY AND INFORMATION SCIENCE

Volume 100

THE *USMARC FORMAT FOR HOLDINGS AND LOCATIONS*

THE *USMARC FORMAT FOR HOLDINGS AND LOCATIONS*
Development, Implementation and Use

Edited by
BARRY B. BAKER

LONDON AND NEW YORK

First published in 1988 by The Haworth Press, Inc.

This edition first published in 2020
by Routledge
2 Park Square, Milton Park, Abingdon, Oxon OX14 4RN

and by Routledge
52 Vanderbilt Avenue, New York, NY 10017

Routledge is an imprint of the Taylor & Francis Group, an informa business

© 1988 The Haworth Press, Inc.

All rights reserved. No part of this book may be reprinted or reproduced or utilised in any form or by any electronic, mechanical, or other means, now known or hereafter invented, including photocopying and recording, or in any information storage or retrieval system, without permission in writing from the publishers.

Trademark notice: Product or corporate names may be trademarks or registered trademarks, and are used only for identification and explanation without intent to infringe.

British Library Cataloguing in Publication Data
A catalogue record for this book is available from the British Library

ISBN: 978-0-367-34616-4 (Set)
ISBN: 978-0-429-34352-0 (Set) (ebk)
ISBN: 978-0-367-36040-5 (Volume 100) (hbk)
ISBN: 978-0-429-34350-6 (Volume 100) (ebk)

Publisher's Note
The publisher has gone to great lengths to ensure the quality of this reprint but points out that some imperfections in the original copies may be apparent.

Disclaimer
The publisher has made every effort to trace copyright holders and would welcome correspondence from those they have been unable to trace.

The *USMARC Format for Holdings and Locations:* Development, Implementation and Use

Barry B. Baker
Editor

The Haworth Press
New York • London

The USMARC Format for Holdings and Locations: *Development, Implementation and Use* is monographic supplement #2 to the journal *Technical Services Quarterly*. It is not supplied as part of the subscription to the journal, but is available from the publisher at an additional charge.

© 1988 by The Haworth Press, Inc. All rights reserved. No part of this work may be reproduced or utilized in any form or by any means, electronic or mechanical, including photocopying, microfilm and recording or by any information storage and retrieval system, without permission in writing from the publisher. Printed in the United States of America.

The Haworth Press, Inc., 12 West 32 Street, New York, NY 10001
EUROSPAN/Haworth, 3 Henrietta Street, WC2E 8LU England

LIBRARY OF CONGRESS
Library of Congress Cataloging-in-Publication Data

The USMARC format for holdings and locations : development, implementation, and use / Barry B. Baker, editor.
   p.   cm. — (Monographic supplement to the journal Technical services quarterly, ISSN 0897-8425 ; #2)
   Includes bibliographical references and index.
   ISBN 0-86656-695-3
   1. USMARC format for holdings and locations. 2. MARC System — United States — Format. 3. Holdings (Bibliographic data) — Standards — United States. 4. Serials control systems — Automation — Standards — United States. 5. Catalogs, Union — Automation — Standards — United States. 6. Catalogs, On-line — Standards — United States. 7. Machine-readable bibliographic data — Standards — United States. 8. Exchange of bibliographic information — Automation — Standards — United States. I. Baker, Barry B. II. Series.
Z699.4.M2U753   1988
025.3'0285 — dc19   88-16383
                                                                                          CIP

CONTENTS

Introduction   1
Barry B. Baker

Developing a Format for Holdings and Location Data   3
Nolan F. Pope

SOLINET's Implementation of the *USMARC Format for
Holdings and Locations*   39
Michele I. Dalehite

Implementation of the *USMARC Format for Holdings and
Locations* at the Harvard University Library   61
Priscilla L. Caplan

Implementation and Use of the *USMARC Format for
Holdings and Locations* at the University of
Georgia Libraries   79
Greg Anderson

Adapting the *USMARC Format for Holdings and Locations*
for Local Serials Control: The University of Kansas
Serials System   99
John S. Miller

VTLS Serials Control: Using the *USMARC Format for
Holdings and Locations* in an Integrated, Online System   123
*Charles A. Litchfield III
Deborah H. McGrath*

Implementation of the *USMARC Format for Holdings and
Locations* at the University of Florida Libraries   137
Nancy Lynne Williams

Faxon Serial Interfaces: Implementation of the *USMARC Format for Holdings and Locations* for Serials Check-in and Union List   143
Mary Ellen Clapper

The NOTIS Implementation of the *USMARC Format for Holdings and Locations*   173
Peggy Steele

The Display of Serial Holdings Statements   191
Marjorie E. Bloss

SISAC: The Serials Industry Systems Advisory Committee   215
Minna C. Saxe

Index   229

Introduction

The newest member of the MARC Format family is the *US-MARC Format for Holdings and Locations*. Presently in a "Final Draft," the Format has already had a significant impact on libraries. As the other MARC Formats have had a great impact on automation in libraries, so will this new format, but in an area where others feared to tread: the World of Serials Control.

As an infant in the MARC Format family, this new format has been the source of many varied and frequent discussions among librarians as they seek answers to such questions as: Just what exactly is this new format? How and why was it developed? How is it to be used? Is it complicated to use? What libraries are using it? How is the 866 field to be used? What about pattern information in the 853 field? Should a national database of publication pattern information be established? These are but a few of the questions and issues discussed in this volume.

The Format was developed for serials holdings statements; however, it is currently being reviewed for its ability to handle other holdings data as well. It was initially developed as part of a project to develop a database of holdings and bibliographic information by eight member libraries of the Southeastern Association of Research Libraries (SEARL).

In October, 1981, these libraries were awarded an Office of Education Title II-C grant to promote resource sharing of research materials and in particular, current serials. Those institutions were: Emory University, University of Florida, Florida State University, University of Georgia, University of Kentucky, University of Miami, University of Tennessee, and Virginia Polytechnic Institute and State University. Other libraries joined the original eight during later phases of the grant.

This cooperative program was also to include development of

1

serials selection/deselection projects and improved interlibrary loan procedures. Identified as an important factor in the program was the development of an automated system for the manipulation of serials holdings information so serials resources could be shared more easily. Obviously, it was important to have a database of detailed serials holdings information available. Thus, machine manipulation of such a database became important and development of a method to communicate such data began.

It soon became apparent that there was a need for a national standard, and the Library of Congress was asked to participate. A committee was established to develop the Format. This is chronicled here in Nolan Pope's paper, in the introduction to the *USMARC Format for Holdings and Locations* itself, and in an article by Linda Sapp Visk published in the Winter, 1985 (Vol. 21, No. 1) issue of *Drexel Library Quarterly*.

While this volume records the development of the Format, it more importantly looks at how the Format has been implemented and how difficult issues of interpretation have been handled. It is also concerned with how the Format is being used on a daily basis.

Many times during our work to implement the Format at the University of Georgia Libraries, we wondered how other libraries were handling a particular problem or interpreting a certain requirement. The existence of a volume such as this would have been very helpful to us. That was the basis for this volume.

The papers included have been written by individuals who have firsthand experience with the Format. These authors were, as it is frequently said these days, "on the cutting edge." Their experience with the use of the Format, the NISO Standards, and the SISAC code will provide the reader with an introduction to the Format and information on how other institutions approached the application of the Format to their situations.

Barry B. Baker
Assistant Director for Technical Services
University of Georgia Libraries

Developing a Format for Holdings and Location Data

Nolan F. Pope

Serials location and holdings information are critical aspects of any catalog information, whether printed or online, and serials themselves are a growing segment of library holdings. Andrew Osburn has chronicled a continual increase in serial publications since 1700, with the growth in the twentieth century described as phenomenal.[1]

The development of a machine-readable format for such location and holdings data must consider its relationship to other types of data, such as bibliographic records; its relationship to the National Information Standards Organization (NISO) Z39 standards; the structure of the format itself; the specific fields which are necessary to support various types of applications dealing with serial holdings and location information; and the flexibility of the format. That flexibility is best seen in the options for selecting the level of recording appropriate for a specific application or product.

As noted in the *USMARC Format for Holdings and Locations*,[2] published by the Library of Congress, information describing a library's materials is defined in three categories: bibliographic, authority, and local holdings. While the first two are relatively clear in definition, the latter is not. Local holdings information may describe a specific copy of the item held by an institution, may consist of information that is peculiar to the institution itself, or may provide information needed for internal processing and maintenance of the material. Given these variations, local information may be de-

---

Nolan F. Pope is Associate Director for Automation, University of Wisconsin Libraries, Madison.

3

fined as copy specific data, institution specific data, and local processing data.

The *USMARC Format for Holdings and Locations* defines data which would be related to these categories and provides specific tags to identify them. Applications using the Format may use as many of the data elements as necessary to satisfy their requirements. Also, since it is a communications format, it does not include some data elements which may be used in designing automated system functional capabilities.

However, in accordance with the underlying principles of the USMARC Formats,[3] the Format does not define local fields. The MARC principles define certain categories of tags as being reserved for local definition; it is these fields and their subfields which some application software packages will develop to support internal or local data needed for the application involved.

When the Format was initially being written, the primary concern and impetus for the format was serial holdings. While there has been analysis and consideration of its use for other formats, this paper will primarily address its support of holdings data for serial publications. In that regard, the following definitions of serial holdings are used.

Summary Holdings refers to data formatted according to the American National Standard for Serial Holdings Statements at the Summary Level, Z39.42-1980. This Standard was published in 1980; has since been subsumed as levels of Z39.44, the new standard for summary and detailed serial holdings information; and has been used for many union lists since that time, including OCLC's Union List capabilities.

Perhaps most significant in this notation is that material is recorded, primarily, only at the highest level of enumeration and chronology; there are no captions; the notation is open-ended; and volumes which are 50% complete are noted as complete, while those less than 50% complete are noted as totally missing.

Detailed Summary Holdings refers to material recorded at a summary level but with sufficient detail to show specifically which issues are held and which are missing. Detailed Summary Holdings contain the specificity defined in the Z39.44 level 4, which contains enumeration and chronology information. This standard was published in 1986 after considerable discussion and distribution of various drafts.

Piece Level Holdings refers to data representing a physical piece of the holdings information. Data elements relate to one physical piece, and an individual field or group of fields is used to define each piece. It should be noted that while such information may be maintained by the Format, it is not necessary to record or to store enumeration/chronology data at this level.

Copy Level Holdings refers to a specific copy of a title's holdings. Copy may be defined according to local definitions. For example, a title may have initial volumes in microform and later volumes in print. This may be defined as copy 1 for each, or as copy 1 and copy 2. This relates to the local practice of using a new copy number when location information changes, such as microform room as opposed to stacks.

Composite Holdings designates holdings for the institution, at a composite level, to show its entire holdings coverage. Such information can be recorded into the Format, or if all necessary fields and subfields are present, multiple copy holdings notations at the local system level can be compressed to a single notation which shows the institution's total holdings with no indication of overlap between copies or the division of copies between multiple locations.

Compressed Holdings refers to holdings which have been combined beyond the physical piece level of holdings information. They may be condensed to levels defined in the NISO Z39 standards or to a level which is locally defined. It is important to note that compressed holdings may continue to show specific details of holdings, recording down to the lowest level of enumeration and chronology those items which are held and which are missing.

BACKGROUND

The development of the *USMARC Format for Holdings and Locations* evolved from plans of the Southeastern Association for Research Libraries (SEARL) for a regional resource sharing program, primarily for serials.[4] Using a database of bibliographic and holdings information of the serial holdings in those libraries, it would be

6   THE USMARC FORMAT FOR HOLDINGS AND LOCATIONS

possible to establish areas of responsibilities, building on existing holdings. While the program would include other aspects of resource sharing, a major premise was the need to establish holdings in a machine-readable format which would facilitate this program. Plans included the definition of such a format, anticipating that machine-manipulation of the resulting holdings database could show areas of strengths and gaps in holdings within the region.

In 1981, eight Southeastern ARL libraries[5] received an Office of Education Title II-C grant to begin the development of a regional serials system for resource sharing. While the project was a regional one, it was realized that the lack of a machine-readable standard for serial holdings data was of concern to the entire library community. Library automation efforts had long circumvented many serial control issues due to their complexity and the desire to avoid development which might later be contradicted by a standard which would differ from that local development. In particular, serials check-in and control systems needed such a format to support both prediction and flexibility in future displays of that data.

Upon receipt of the grant, the Southeastern ARL libraries asked the Library of Congress to participate in the development of such a format. Given the need for a standard format for serial holdings data and recognizing the leadership role of the Library of Congress in the area of MARC Formats, it was felt that their participation would assist in meeting the requirements of other libraries and help in submitting the product to the national review process to establish a MARC Format.

The Library of Congress accepted the invitation and the following committee was constituted: David Bishop, University of Georgia; Gary K. McCone, Library of Congress; Anton R. Pierce, Virginia Polytechnic Institute and State University; Nolan F. Pope, University of Florida; Mary S. Price, Library of Congress; Linda Sapp Visk, Emory University; and Elaine Woods, Consultant and project manager for the Southeastern ARL Cooperative Serials Project.

The Committee began its work by reviewing data elements of holdings data as defined in existing applications of automated serials systems, cooperative purchasing files, union lists including newspaper holdings, interlibrary loan systems, and the relevant

NISO Z39 work. While few sophisticated, comprehensive serial control systems existed at that time, numerous developments had addressed various aspects of the issues being analyzed by the Committee. Many libraries, agencies, bibliographic utilities, and companies were supportive and helpful by providing detailed information and specifications on their own work.

The Committee analyzed the data into two groups:

- that which was relevant to holdings and location data, thus being important for communication with other systems,
- and that which was solely important for local processing and thus not important for communication.

The goal of the Committee was to establish a communications format, as with the MARC bibliographic formats. It was never perceived as a format which would support all local processing applications.

The Committee established a number of working assumptions which led to a set of functional specifications. Several working draft formats were created and tested against a set of library records to determine their feasibility. After a final draft was tested at several Southeastern ARL libraries and at the Library of Congress, areas of clarification were added to the draft which was then mailed to a number of institutions and individuals for comment.

In October, 1982, the draft was presented to the USMARC Advisory Group. In November, 1982, it was reviewed extensively by 33 invited participants at a three day conference on the format. After incorporating the comments and suggestions from these reviews, the draft was reviewed at subsequent meetings of the MARBI Committee and the USMARC Advisory Group in June and September of 1983. Receiving final draft status from those groups, the Format was published by the Library of Congress in December, 1984 as a Final Draft. Following sufficient testing and application, the format will receive another future review by those groups. The Library of Congress and the MARBI Committee have continued to receive comments and discuss reactions to the format. As with the MARC bibliographic format, the MARBI Committee began in 1986 to ac-

8 THE USMARC FORMAT FOR HOLDINGS AND LOCATIONS

cept proposals for enhancements and changes to the *USMARC Format for Holdings and Locations*.

In developing the format, numerous issues were confronted. However, three became more basic and central to the overall design of the format. First, the scope of the data to be included was a fundamental question. Discussion centered on various types of local information versus that related specifically to holdings and location data. While it was recognized that various systems and applications would need additional data elements, it was decided that the communications format would be more efficient to carry only those elements related to the holdings and location data and to the processing of that data.

Second, the committee considered the issue of separate versus embedded record formats. The embedded format approach would add fields to the existing bibliographic formats; separate record formats would create separate, unique records which would be linked to the bibliographic record.

Feeling that holdings records for multivolume materials would be more easily supported and manipulated as separate records, the Committee first developed the format using a separate record concept. It was then analyzed to determine how it could be embedded into bibliographic record data. The result is a format which stands alone as a separate record format but can also optionally embed holdings and location data in bibliographic formats under certain conditions.

The third major concern of the Committee was the complexity of the format and the ease of use. The goal was a format which would be easy to use and economical, yet sophisticated and flexible enough to support various types of applications.

The resulting format allows local options in determining the level of recording to be used. Yet the necessity of supporting displays according to the *American National Standard for Information Sciences – Serial Holding Statements* (ANSI Z39.44-1986),[6] added elements to the format. The same is true in allowing the data elements to be embedded into a single record for the bibliographic and the physical or holdings data.

RELATIONSHIP TO BIBLIOGRAPHIC RECORDS

As noted previously, the issue of using a separate holdings format record as opposed to embedding the holdings and location data into the bibliographic format was a major concern. It seems important to consider further the issues related to this concern; these affect both the creation and maintenance of the data as well as the processing of the data by automated systems.

Arguments favoring a separate format are:

1. Holdings data are far more dynamic than bibliographic data. Updating of holdings would be more efficient using a separate format.
2. Updates to holdings records can be communicated without the necessity of communicating the bibliographic record.
3. A separate format would allow record replacement for record update. Since the bibliographic record has no technique of indicating which field has changed, holdings updates to the bibliographic record with embedded holdings would complicate catalog maintenance.
4. A separate record would eliminate excessively long records that would result from having both bibliographic and holdings data in a single format. This length would create problems for many existing systems.
5. The bibliographic record could be communicated without having to remove the holdings data when so desired. This would be particularly true if the receiving systems do not support the *USMARC Format for Holdings and Locations*.
6. Copy-specific data could be handled more easily in a separate format.
7. Piece-specific data for serials cannot be adequately treated within the framework of the bibliographic record.

Arguments opposing a separate format are:

1. A comparatively large amount of overhead is necessary when communicating holdings for nonserial material such as mono-

graphs. The same would be true for serials recorded at levels 1 or 2 as defined by the NISO Z39.44.

2. There would be difficulty in linking holdings records with the appropriate bibliographic record in intersystem communication.

These points, as noted in the Format document, led to a separate format with the option for creating holdings and location data as embedded fields of the bibliographic record format when certain conditions exist.

The most basic conditions are that separate holdings records are required for each copy when enumeration and chronology are recorded and when specification of the physical form is required for a copy, i.e., a different field 007 (Physical Description) is needed.

Multiple holdings records may be linked to a single bibliographic record (Figure 1). A separate record should be created when location and call number information change. A single holdings record can be used to show changes in publication pattern data and captions as well as gaps in the enumeration and chronology of a copy's holdings.

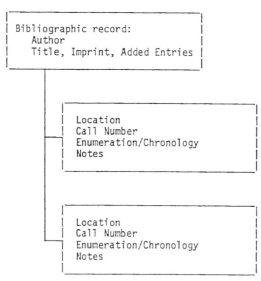

FIGURE 1. Record Structure

A holdings record can be created for each copy or as a composite holdings statement for the institution. This decision would depend upon the use of the records. For some interlibrary loan applications or resource sharing agreements, it may be adequate to simply know who has a range of holdings, regardless of form, location, number of copies, and overlap or gaps between those copies.

The Format also recognizes that library practices vary regarding the recording of holdings for print and microform copies of a title. While *AACR2* requires separate bibliographic records, each with their own holdings statements, for print and for microform holdings of a title, earlier cataloging rules did not. Also, many libraries have continued their practice of showing all holdings together, regardless of format.

The *USMARC Format for Holdings and Locations* supports either approach. Naturally, separate MARC holdings records can be attached to different bibliographic records. It is also possible to link multiple holdings records, each representing different formats, to the same bibliographic record. To support this, the 007 field (Physical Description) is repeated in the holdings record since those features relate to a specific copy. For libraries using different bibliographic records for print and microform copies, this would also support separate designations of microform masters, polarity, or emulsions, linked to a single bibliographic record.

The 007 field is an exact duplication of that defined for the bibliographic formats. The 008 field (Fixed Length Data Elements — General Information) is a duplicate field tag but the values defined are unique to the Holdings and Location Format. The same applies to the record leader. For embedded records, since the bibliographic record's leader and 008 would then apply to the bibliographic data, the values in these holdings record fields are transferred to unique fields which are also embedded.

The fields which contain the location, call number, publication pattern, and the enumeration and chronology are unique field tags for this Format. This approach obviously facilitates embedding of the holdings and location information in the bibliographic record when desirable.

The *USMARC Format for Holdings and Locations* contains various linking numbers to show relationships between bibliographic and holdings information. Those numbers which are also contained in the bibliographic formats have retained their same field tags:

010	Library of Congress Control Number (LCCN)
020	International Standard Book Number (ISBN)
022	International Standard Serial Number (ISSN)
023	Standard Film Number
024	Standard Recording Number
027	Standard Technical Report Number (STRN)
030	CODEN Designation
035	System Control Numbers

The format also developed a new tag, the 014 (Linkage Number) to establish a format for linking holdings records to the bibliographic records of the major bibliographic utilities and networks, i.e., the numbers of the 001 and the 004 fields for the specified network.

The Format contains fields for many types of local, copy level data. Additional elements which would be used for local maintenance, for local system processing, or for support of additional applications related to copy level data could be added to the holdings record rather than to the bibliographic level.

APPLICATION ISSUES AND EXTENT OF USE

The *USMARC Format for Holdings and Locations* defines data elements of holdings and location information which would be relevant for communication to other systems or agencies. In developing the Format, numerous types of applications were considered and many fields relate to a specific type of use of that data.

While a library might choose to code all the various possible data elements, an application might choose to communicate or use only a subset of those elements. The same would apply to the ability to segregate the data according to location, format or level of recording.

One of the most obvious uses of the Format is to support holdings and location information for an online catalog or for a serials union list, whether online or output to another physical format. Design of the Format considered its ability to facilitate maintenance of that data as well as flexibility in display options. As with bibliographic data coded according to the MARC formats, the data can be displayed according to the specifications of a given system yet retained in a standard format for communicating to other systems which might change the display or combine the data for display with records from another source.

The Format contains the fields which would be necessary to develop a serials control system, including serials prediction for the check-in function. Subfields are also defined which would allow individual check-in records to be merged or compressed into a detailed summary holdings statement.

Many applications are more concerned with the physical piece rather than the bibliographic piece, such as circulation and preservation. The subfields allow designation of both physical and bibliographic items, including a subfield for the barcode. Thus a system could use the format for the circulation item record which could then be compressed into the detailed summary holdings record. Such programming still remains complex, but the elements needed to link these applications are provided.

RELATIONSHIP TO Z39.44 STANDARD FOR SERIAL HOLDINGS STATEMENTS

At the beginning of the work to develop the *USMARC Format for Holdings and Locations*, it was apparent that the NISO standards for serial holdings must be supported. This meant that each element defined in the Z39 standards must also be defined in the MARC Format. This decision controlled many of the data elements defined in the 008 of the Holdings and Location Format.

When the development of the MARC format began, there was one existing Z39 standard and another in development. The first was the *Standard for Serial Holdings Statements at the Summary Level*, published in 1980 as ANSI Z39.42. This standard, which had been used for many union list projects and for the OCLC union

14   THE USMARC FORMAT FOR HOLDINGS AND LOCATIONS

listing, called for recording the enumeration and chronology at the highest level only, except where ambiguity would result. The 50% rule for showing a title as being either complete or entirely missing — depending upon being above or below the 50% mark — was to eliminate the need for showing lower levels of data. Since data was recorded only at the highest levels of enumeration, there were no captions. That Standard also included many coded values which could optionally be used alone, recording no enumeration and chronology information.

In 1979, ANSI Z39 appointed the Subcommittee E: Serial Holdings Statements at the Detailed Level. The work of this committee produced a draft standard which allowed recording of holdings data at the detailed summary level, meaning that all levels of enumeration and chronology were reported. It also called for reporting both the beginning and ending enumeration/chronology for a holdings statement; the Z39.42 endorsed open-ended statements.

As a result of the library community's criticism of having two disparate serial display standards, the Z39 Program Committee held a meeting of the Subcommittee E members with those of Subcommittee 40 who had written the earlier standard. Also attending were the members of the Holdings Committee of the Southeastern ARL Serials Project, who were working on the *USMARC Format for Holdings and Locations*, and other representatives of the user community. It was recommended, and later approved by Z39, that there be a single Z39 for serial holdings and that the Subcommittee E be charged with its development. Subcommittee E was renamed Subcommittee E: Serial Holdings Statements.

The resulting Z39.44 standard, which was approved in late 1985, thus incorporates various levels of reporting, including those originally covered by the Z39.42 standard. All of those levels are supported by the *USMARC Format for Holdings and Locations*. It is important to note that the Standard defines these levels of recording, not the Format. Use of the Format does not mean that all data elements must be used or that a library must record complete, detailed summary holdings.

While it has been shown in existing applications that the Format can be used to create records according to levels 3 and 4 of the

Z39.44 standard, a library may also choose to record data in the formatted version but generate displays in a form defined locally. Transmitting the formatted data to other agencies for use in other displays, such as union lists, could then translate the formatted data into displays such as the Z39.44 standard. This flexibility parallels that which exists for using MARC bibliographic data in numerous online catalog systems, each with their own display formats for the information.

It should be noted that there is a reverse parallel between the development process of bibliographic and holdings formats and displays for each. Most bibliographic data for large libraries use the MARC Format and did so prior to use of that data for generating online displays from machine-readable records. As a result, automation vendors of online catalogs were able to design their own display screens.

For holdings data, standards and especially machine-readable communication format definitions for the data have been developed after the creation of many online systems. Many variations in the formatting of that data have emerged as applications were implemented. Machine-readable union lists were particularly common, and each defined its own formats for the data. Most all, however, formatted the actual enumeration and chronology information into either a free-text field or used minimal subfielding and coding. Thus, while the data was tagged as identifying the enumeration and chronology, its elements were not formatted for flexibility in manipulating displays of information.

In spite of the existing variations between many machine-readable records containing holdings and location data, it was felt that the future amount of data would be even greater. Holdings is the missing component in many resource databases, especially at the detailed level. A standard format which could support the display of that data as well as the serials control applications, with the ability to transfer the receipt data from serials control into an updated detailed summary statement, would be very significant.

Also, the previous change in standards for recording serial holdings information indicated a need for formatted data which could later be reformatted according to rule changes.

16   *THE USMARC FORMAT FOR HOLDINGS AND LOCATIONS*

Given these realizations, the Format was designed to support existing machine-readable holdings and location data as well as future data which could be input according to the format tagging definitions. Existing data could be held as free-text fields or could be machine-converted to a formatted version of the data—or something nearly so, depending on whether all the data elements existed and were appropriately designated in the earlier records.

FORMAT STRUCTURE AND FIELD DEFINITIONS

The *USMARC Format for Holdings and Locations* is designed to stand as a separate record or to be embedded within a bibliographic record, as discussed previously. This paper, however, will focus on the Format as a separate record and concentrate on the relationship of fields and subfields and the flexibility they provide.

Each holdings record has its own record leader, as does a bibliographic record in the USMARC Formats. The leader values are defined for the holdings record and are primarily used in the processing of that record by automated systems.

There are two fixed length fields: the 008 and the 007. The holdings record has its own 008 field. The values of each position in that field are defined in the format and relate only to the holdings record, not to the bibliographic record. Some of these data elements relate to the coded values of the NISO Z39 serials standard. Other elements are used primarily for the processing of these records.

The 007 in the holdings record is a duplicate of the 007 from the bibliographic record. Since the information contained in the 007 is actually copy specific, it is necessary to retain the data at this level. For example, the type of microform or the speed of a sound recording may vary with each copy, yet the bibliographic record is the same for all copies linked to it. For libraries who attach print and microform copies to a single bibliographic record, the 007 must be held in the holdings record showing the microform holdings—not in the bibliographic record which governs all attached holdings information.

Control Numbers

The holdings format contains a number of linking fields. These are the numeric fields, such as the ISSN, LCCN, CODEN, and others which are also defined for the bibliographic formats. These have been repeated in the holdings record using the same format definitions as in the bibliographic records.

These fields are present to support linking of holdings and bibliographic records. Various systems may link the bibliographic and holdings records differently. Some applications may update the holdings records via these numbers, may use these numbers in combining records from numerous sources, or may use these as access points to holdings data. It should also be possible for applications to add these numbers to holdings records if the values appear in the bibliographic records, avoiding duplicate entry of the values for original input. In most cases they will likely be stored in the bibliographic record and only used in the holdings records when communicating holdings records for linking and merging data in other systems.

The 014 has been defined as a "Linkage Number" to contain the record number of bibliographic utilities such as OCLC and the RLIN system of the Research Libraries Group. The 035 then exists for local numbers, as has been allowed in the bibliographic formats. Considering the multitude of uses which have been applied to the 035, creating a separate field for the bibliographic utility record numbers allows more efficient processing of links between bibliographic and holdings records using those record sources.

Location and Call Number

The field 852, titled "Location/Call Number," contains those elements of data plus others which relate to that level of information. Specifically, the elements of information would apply to all materials held at that location under that call number (Figure 2).

The first indicator of the 852 shows the classification type of the call number used in the field. That information could be used for creating call number lists of records. The second indicator provides

18   *THE USMARC FORMAT FOR HOLDINGS AND LOCATIONS*

```
852  LOCATION/CALL NUMBER    [R]

     INDICATORS

               Indicator 1 - Type of classification/shelving scheme

          ß         No information provided
          Ø         Library of Congress classification scheme
          1         Dewey Decimal classification scheme
          2         National Library of Medicine scheme
          3         Superintendent of Documents (GPO) scheme
          4         Shelved by shelving control number
          5         Shelved by title
          6         Classed separately
          8         Other

               Indicator 2 - Number/location relationship

          ß         No information provided
          Ø         Not shelved by enumeration
          1         Shelved by primary enumeration
          2         Shelved by alternative enumeration

     SUBFIELDS

          $a        Institution/location  [NR]
          $b        Sublocation/collection  [R]
          $c        Shelving location  [R]
          $d        Name of individual collector [NR]
          $e        Address of collector  [R]
          $f        Location qualifier (coded)  [R]
          $g        Location qualifier (non-coded)  [R]
          $h        Classification number  [NR]
          $i        Item number (book number)  [R]
          $j        Shelving control number  [NR]
          $k        Call number prefix/suffix  [R]
          $l        Shelving form of title  [NR]
          $p        Physical item/piece identification  [NR]
          $q        Physical condition (piece level)  [NR]
          $r        Preservation status  [NR]
          $s        Copyright article code  [R]
          $t        Copy number(s)  [NR]
          $z        Note  [R]
```

FIGURE 2

information as to the shelving rules governing the material. For example, within call number, are the materials shelved by primary or alternative enumeration?

For location, the format allows multiple subdivisions of location information, reflecting a hierarchy if appropriate. The lower levels of location information are repeatable, allowing a library to define its own degree of complexity in terms of hierarchical sublocations.

The call number is divided between classification number and book number. For call numbers with multiple segments but no designation of classification and book number, or where these are not the elements of the call number, the $i is repeatable. This is somewhat parallel to the formatting of the OCLC 099 field which contains repeatable $a designations.

The subfield $k can be used to create a prefix or suffix to a call number, paralleling the use of bracketed information before and after the 049 code in the OCLC system. The positioning of the $k before or after the call number subfields indicates if it is used as prefix or suffix.

Subfield $1 may be used to indicate the shelving form of title when classification numbers are not used. This may reflect the actual title on the bound volumes and be important in locating materials.

For applications requiring the recording of the data at the physical piece level, the $p of the 852 may be used to note a barcode number or an accession number. It should be clarified, however, that this data element is used in the 852 for single physical piece items. Multipiece materials, which would have an 863 field to show enumeration and chronology, would have to record the $p information in the 863 field, linking it to a specific physical piece.

The 863 field, which will be discussed later, is used to record the actual enumeration and chronology of materials held under the location and call number of the 852 field.

The 852 $t is used to record copy numbers of materials which do not require use of the 863 field. While the $t may be used to show a range of copy numbers, it cannot use punctuation to show gaps in the numbering; separate 852 fields are required to make that notation. This requirement is due to the processing of that data to generate accurate punctuation.

However, the field does not restrict or set parameters on copy numbering practices. If a serial's holdings are split between two locations but viewed as both being part of copy 1 since there is a single subscription, there are simply two 852 fields, each having the same value in the $t. Each 852 would contain its own location and call number.

The last subfield of the 852 is $z, a note field.[7] This is used to

20 THE USMARC FORMAT FOR HOLDINGS AND LOCATIONS

record notes which apply to a specific copy or set of copies identified in that 852. Notes which apply to a specific volume within a copy's holdings, for example, would be included in the 863 field, not in the 852 $z.

Enumeration/Chronology Data and Publication Patterns

The next set of fields and subfields reflect the most complex aspects of serial holdings data: the enumeration, the chronology, and the publication pattern information. These elements are defined and formatted to allow manipulation of the data to generate displays and to support automated functions such as serials check-in.

It is important to repeat a basic premise mentioned initially. Not all subfields in the enumeration, chronology, and publication pattern fields are required. Many subfields relate only to specific applications using the format. Also, it is possible to record historically the holdings data for a title with one level of detail, and then begin to record future acquisitions at a different level as automated systems become available to support that encoding. This flexibility for dealing with existing holdings information as well as future holdings notations was an important principle in the development of the Format.

In looking at the fields' holdings enumeration, chronology, and publication pattern information, it is important to understand the relationship between fields as well as their independent function. These fields exist in groups. The 853 field (Figure 4) contains the publication pattern and caption information for a set of holdings. The enumeration and chronology data elements for that set of holdings are recorded in the 863 field (Figure 5).

This results in a pairing of 853 and 863 fields (Figure 3)[8] to show the publication pattern, including captions for the enumeration, and the actual enumeration and chronology which it governs. For complex holding statements, the 863 is repeatable, meaning that there can be many 863 fields related to a single 853 field. This may continue until there is a change in the publication pattern. When that happens, a new 853 field is required to show the new publication

Nolan F. Pope

853/863 Pairs

```
852 01 $a DLC   $b Ser Div   $h A123 $i .B45 $z Gift

853 01 $6 1   $a v.   $b no.   $i (year)   $j (month)


863 40 $6 1.1   $a 1-10   $i 1970-1979
863 40 $6 1.2   $a 12   $b 1-6   $i 1981   $j 01-06
863 40 $6 1.3   $a 13-14   $i 1982-1983
```

```
Holdings:  Library has:   Volumes 1-10
                          Volume 12, Numbers 1-6
                          Volumes 13-14
```

This example, to show the pairing of 853 and 863 fields, does not use all
subfields which show the complete publication pattern information, such as the
number of issues per volume.

FIGURE 3

pattern. Subsequent holdings are then recorded in new 863 fields linked to that publication pattern information.

Application software, such as that for an online catalog or a union list database, would create displays by combining the captions in the 853 with the enumeration/chronology of the 863 to produce a holdings statement. For a serials control application with serials check-in capabilities, the publication pattern information in the 853 would be used to predict next issues or identify missing issues.

The 853 and 863 groups of fields are used to reflect information relating to the basic bibliographic unit. For holdings related to supplements and accompanying materials, a different set of fields is used: the 854 and 864. Consistent with those fields, the 854 defines the publication pattern and the 864 contains the enumeration and chronology. A parallel set of fields is also included for indexes: the 855 and 865. Later discussion will show the necessity for a separate set of fields and the processing of that information for creating displays or serials control applications.

22 THE USMARC FORMAT FOR HOLDINGS AND LOCATIONS

```
853  DEFINITION OF ENUMERATION AND CHRONOLOGY/PUBLICATION PATTERN FOR
     BASIC BIBLIOGRAPHIC UNIT   [R]

     INDICATORS

             Indicator 1 - Compressability/Expandability
         Ø       Cannot be compressed or expanded
         1       Can be compressed but not expanded
         2       Can be compressed and expanded
         3       Unknown

             Indicator 2 - Completeness/verification of data
         Ø       Captions verified; all levels present
         1       Captions verified; all levels may not be present
         2       Captions unverified; all levels present
         3       Captions unverified; all levels may not be present


     SUBFIELDS

         $6       Sequence Control Number (SCN)  [NR]
         $a       Term designating first (highest) level of enumeration  [NR]
         $b       Term designating second level of enumeration  [NR]
         $c       Term designating third level of enumeration  [NR]
         $d       Term designating fourth level of enumeration  [NR]
         $e       Term designating fifth level of enumeration  [NR]
         $f       Term designating sixth level of enumeration  [NR]
         $g       Term designating alternative numbering scheme,
                    first level of enumeration  [NR]
         $h       Term designating alternative numbering scheme,
                    second level of enumeration  [NR]
         $i       Term designating first (highest) level of chronology  [NR]
         $j       Term designating second level of chronology  [NR]
         $k       Term designating third level of chronology  [NR]
         $1       Term designating fourth level of chronology  [NR]
         $m       Term designating alternative numbering scheme,
                    chronology  [NR]
         $t       Term designating copy  [NR]
         $u       Bibliographic units per next higher level  [R]
         $v       Restart/continuous numbering code  [R]
         $w       Issues per year/frequency  [NR]
         $x       Calendar change  [NR]
         $y       Regularity pattern  [NR]
         $3       Definition data span  [NR]
```

FIGURE 4

The 853 and 863 Fields

The Indicators

These fields contain many subfields, and in many cases, there is
a parallel between a given subfield of the two fields. First, how-

Nolan F. Pope 23

863 ENUMERATION AND CHRONOLOGY -- BASIC BIBLIOGRAPHIC UNITS [R]

INDICATORS

Indicator 1 - Level of specificity
ɮ   Level of specificity not specified
3   Holdings, level 3
4   Holdings, level 4
5   Holdings, level 4, with physical piece designation

Indicator 2 - Form of holdings
ɮ   Form of holdings not specified
Ø   Compressed
1   Uncompressed (single item)
2   Compressed, use alternative display
3   Uncompressed, use alternative display
4   Item(s) not published

SUBFIELDS

$6	Sequence Control Number (SCN) [NR]
$a	First (highest) level of enumeration [NR]
$b	Second level of enumeration [NR]
$c	Third level of enumeration [NR]
$d	Fourth level of enumeration [NR]
$e	Fifth level of enumeration [NR]
$f	Sixth level of enumeration [NR]
$g	Alternative numbering scheme, first level of enumeration [NR]
$h	Alternative numbering scheme, second level of enumeration [NR]
$i	First (highest) level of chronology [NR]
$j	Second level of chronology [NR]
$k	Third level of chronology [NR]
$l	Fourth level of chronology [NR]
$m	Alternative numbering scheme, chronology [NR]
$n	Converted gregorian year [NR]
$p	Physical item/piece designation [NR]
$q	Physical condition (piece level) [NR]
$r	Preservation status [NR]
$s	Copyright article code [R]
$t	Copy number [NR]
$w	Gap/non-gap break indicator [NR]
$z	Note [R]

FIGURE 5

ever, it is important to understand the role of the indicators of the 853 and 863 fields for processing the subfield information.

The indicators are used to assist the compressing or expanding of the data by machine processing. Compressing is defined as the process of taking multiple holdings statements and combining them

24 THE USMARC FORMAT FOR HOLDINGS AND LOCATIONS

into a summary or "compressed" report. Expanding would reverse that process, creating an issue-by-issue reporting of holdings from an encoded compressed report. The assumption is that data may be encoded at either level and the machine-processing can translate it into the other, given all the necessary subfields of data elements.

Using this definition of "compress" and "expand," the first indicator of the 853 indicates whether or not the data can be compressed or expanded. Since it is impossible to compress publication pattern data held in that field, this indicator is defining whether the necessary data elements are present in the 853 which would be required to compress or expand the holdings information which is actually held in the 863 field.

The second indicator of the 863 field notes the current status of the enumeration and chronology data recorded in that 863 field. Specifically, is it recorded at a compressed level, such as a summary statement, or at the uncompressed level of detail, possibly with a separate 863 for each issue of a serial?

The use of an indicator for this information is important for the processing of the holdings data into a display format, which may be either a level of the Z39.44 standard or a locally defined format.

It is also these indicators which allow retrospective conversion of holdings data at a compressed level with minimal historical publication pattern information. Assuming a scenario of recording captions but not the actual publication pattern for previous years, the 853 indicator would indicate that there is not complete data to support compression or expansion of the data elements. The indicators of the 863 could indicate the level of detail and of compression which were used to record the enumeration and chronology.

Continuing this scenario, it would be possible to begin creating serial holdings statements as a by-product of a serials control system which predicts arrivals. Since the arrivals would be predicted according to the publication pattern information, the indicator would presumably be set to show that the data to support compression and expansion would be present. Such a system could record the actual receipt by creating a separate 863 field for each issue, meaning that it is totally uncompressed data (Figure 6). Realize, however, that this is simply one scenario. A serials control system

863 Data as Check-in Notation

```
853  $a v.   $b no.  $i (year)  $j (month)

863  $a 10  $b 1  $i 1986  $j 07

863  $a 10  $b 2  $i 1986  $j 08

863  $a 10  $b 3  $i 1986  $j 09

863  $a 10  $b 4  $i 1986  $j 10

863  $a 10  $b 5  $i 1986  $j 11
```

Example shows a separate 863 for each issue of Volume 10 whose issue numbers begin in July of each year. Additional publication pattern subfields are omitted in this example.

FIGURE 6

would not have to create and store a separate 863 field for every issue; that is an application design option.

The second indicator of the 853 defines the completeness and the verification process of the caption data. Again, this will facilitate a notation of varying levels of completeness and verification as would likely occur between retrospective statements and more current holdings statements. If the shelflist or manual records do not indicate exact captions for all levels of enumeration, this allows assumptions without having to verify all captions on the physical pieces. Where appropriate, it also allows libraries to define exact captions and note that they were verified.

To generate displays according to the levels of the NISO Z39 standard for serial holdings information, the first indicator of the 863 field is used to note the level of reporting of data held in that 863 field.

In addition to indicating the Form of Holdings as compressed or uncompressed, the 863 second indicator notes the need for using an "alternate display" rather than that which would result from the data in the 863. Thus the definitions of values 2 and 3:

26 THE USMARC FORMAT FOR HOLDINGS AND LOCATIONS

Indicator 2—Form of holdings.

ƀ Form of holdings not specified

Ø Compressed

1 Uncompressed (single item)

2 Compressed, use alternative display

3 Uncompressed, use alternative display

4 Item(s) not published

Some publication patterns are too complex to be defined within the structure of the 853 and 863 fields. Rather than further complicate the encoding of the data to handle those few exceptions, the 866 field was created to carry either alternative displays of formatted data or free-text displays of data which would not be encoded in any 853/863 type fields.

The 866 will be discussed in more detail later, but it should be realized that the second indicator of the 863 can alert application software to display the text found in the 866 field in place of the data held in that specific 863.

The last value of the second indicator, value 4 for "Items not published," is used to specifically record such items. By explicitly noting these items in separate 863 fields with this indicator, the system could compress the data and create the appropriate punctuation noting gaps and nongap breaks as defined in the Z39 standard. A gap refers to a published item which is missing in an institution's holdings; a nongap refers to a break in the consecutive numbering of a title or volume, as in a publishing irregularity.

The Subfields

The subfields of the 853 and 863 begin with $6. This subfield is used to link the 863 fields of enumeration and chronology data to the appropriate 853 field of publication pattern information.

Subfields $a though $h of the 853 define the captions for the levels of enumeration, with the latter two relating to captions for alternative enumeration, if present. Those same subfields in the 863 field contain the actual enumeration data itself.

Subfields $i through $1 represent the captions for the levels of chronology, if appropriate. Generally, there are no captions for chronology, but the levels of chronology must be defined. In the 863, the same subfields actually contain the chronology data elements.

Figure 7 shows the grouped 853 and 863 fields indicating holdings with two levels of enumeration and chronology.

For items which have chronology but not enumeration, the chronology should be treated as enumeration and recorded in those subfields. In those situations, no data are recorded in the chronology subfields (Figure 8).

Data Compression

The 853 field also contains subfields which identify data elements needed to process the enumeration and chronology data elements. Compression and expansion rely on these values.

```
Multiple Levels of Recording in One Record

    853   03   $6 1   $a v.   $i (year)

    863   40   $6 1.1   $a 1-10   $i 1966-1975

    863   40   $6 1.2   $a 15-20   $i 1980-1985

    853   20   $6 2   $a v.   $b no.   $i (year)   $j (month)

    863   40   $6 2.1   $a 21   $b 1-4   $i 1986   $j 01-04
```

In the first set with one 853 and two 863 fields, data converted from the manual Kardex files are designated as not having the captions verified. Also, since the publication pattern information is not known from that manual record, the first indicator shows that the data cannot be compressed or expanded. The data is considered complete, but the manual records do not indicate the lower levels of publication pattern. Thus they are not recorded.

In the second set of fields, the information is recorded into the format directly rather than from old manual records. Thus, the complete information can be recorded. The indicators show that the data is recorded so that it can be compressed and expanded and that all captions are verified and all levels of enumeration and chronology are recorded.

FIGURE 7

28   THE USMARC FORMAT FOR HOLDINGS AND LOCATIONS

```
Year as Enumeration

    This annual publication is identified only by year.

    853  03  $6 1  $a (year)
    863  40  $ 6.1  $a 1964-1981
```

FIGURE 8

For data to be compressed, 853 subfields $u (bibliographic units per next higher level) and $v (restart/continuous numbering code) must contain precise information.

Subfield $u relates to the number of bibliographic units required to comprise one complete unit at the next higher level. For example, a quarterly publication requires four numbers to make one volume. Compression of this data needs this information to determine if any issues are missing.

The $v which contains the restart or continuous numbering code indicates whether that level has continuously incrementing numbers, or whether the numbering restarts after reaching a certain point. A volume of a monthly publication would contain 12 issues which restart their numbering upon receipt of number 12. Some numbering schemes, especially with alternative numbers, continue in sequence beyond changes in chronology or other definitions. As shown in Figure 9, subfields $u and $v follow the levels of enumeration to which they apply.

Data Expansion

For data to be expanded from a compressed statement to multiple statements, possibly to the extent of an issue-by-issue statement, the subfields $u, $v, $w (the issues per year/frequency), $x (calendar change), and $y (regularity pattern, if applicable) must be present in the field 853. Expansion of the data also requires that all the subfields $a–$m be defined appropriately.

The subfield $w contains coded information as to the frequency of the item. For example, code "q" indicates a quarterly publica-

Nolan F. Pope 29

```
853 Subfields $u and $v


$853  03  $6 1  $a v.  $b no.  $u 12  $c pt.  $u 3

           A serial with 12 numbers per volume and 3 parts
           per number.
```

```
853  03  $6 1  $a v.  $b no.  $u 12  $v c

863  40  $6 1.1  $a 1

863  40  $6 1.2  $a 2  $b 13

           A serial with 12 numbers per volume and
           continuously incrementing issue numbers.
```

```
853  03  $6 1  $a v.  $b no.  $u 12  $v r

863  40  $6 1.1  $a 1

863  40  $6 1.2  $a 2  $b 1

           A serial with 12 numbers per volume and with
           issue numbers that restart with each volume.
```

FIGURE 9

tion. The other field which affects expanding the data is the subfield $x which indicates where the chronological level increments. For example, with a quarterly publication, is number 1 the winter issue or the July issue? (Figure 10).

Additional 863 Subfields

While the data elements following the enumeration and chronology captions in the 853 govern the compressing and expanding of that information, the 863 fields contain subfields which give additional information about that material.

30 *THE USMARC FORMAT FOR HOLDINGS AND LOCATIONS*

```
853 Subfield $w and $x

    Subfield $w.    Frequency Codes.

        a - annual                    i - three times a week
        b - bimonthly (every 2 mo.)   j - three times a month
        c - semiweekly                m - monthly
        d - daily                     q - quarterly
        e - biweekly (every 2 wks)    s - semimonthly
        f - semiannual                t - three times a year
        g - biennial (every 2 yrs)    w - weekly
        h - triennial (every 3 yrs)   x - completely irregular


    Subfield x.   Point of Chronological Level Change.

        01-12      months of year
        21         spring
        22         summer
        23         autumn
        24         winter
```

```
Example:

    853 03 $6 1   $a v. $b no. $u 04 $i (year) $j (month) $w q $x 03

                   Quarterly serial for which issue no. 1 of
                   each volume is dated March.
```

```
Subfield $y is used to designate irregularities in the publication pattern,
such as "monthly except not published in July." The Format document gives a
list of codes which are used to note these irregularities.
```

FIGURE 10

Subfields are present to define the physical piece, to show physical condition and preservation information, copyright article codes, and copy numbers. These apply to the amount of data contained in that 863 field. For example, if the 863 field contains enumeration and chronology data for volumes 1-10, a note on the preservation status would relate to all 10 volumes. An application which needs preservation information on each physical piece would create an

Nolan F. Pope 31

individual 863 for each item and note the preservation data in the subfield $r.[9]

In the latter case, the actual detailed summary holdings statement might appear in an online catalog by compressing the data for the display. However, the system could continue to retain the information encoded in individual 863 fields for preservation control and display that data in staff displays.

The 863 subfield $z is a note field (Figure 11). It applies in the same manner as the preservation field. That is, it relates to all holdings data held in that specific 863.

The subfield $w (Figure 12) contains a designation as to whether the holdings data in an 863 ends with a gap or a nongap break. In some instances, this explicit designation is necessary to provide the system software with adequate information for providing the punc-

```
863 Subfields $r and $z


    863 41  $6 1.1  $a 6  $p 7312986   $r diethyl zinc

            $p shows the piece number of vol. 6

            $r shows the preservation status of vol. 6
```

```
    863 40  $6 1.1  $a 1-10  $i 1910-1919 $z Gift from H. T. Kapps

    863 40  $6 1.2  $a 11-20 $i 1920-1929

        By using two 863 fields, it is possible to note that
        volumes 1-10 are a gift.

        A processing system could optionally create one public
        holdings display statement indicating that the holdings cover
        volumes 1-20, omitting the gift notation.
```

FIGURE 11

32   THE USMARC FORMAT FOR HOLDINGS AND LOCATIONS

```
863 Subfield $w   Gap / non-gap break indicator

Library holds:  1967-1974 and 1976-1984

        853   20   $6 1   $a (year)

        863   40   $6 1.1   $a 1967-1974   $w n

        863   40   $6 1.2   $a 1976-1984

                Value n in $w indicates that the issue for 1975
                was not published, i.e. a non-gap.
```

```
Library holds volumes 1-5
              volume 7, no. 1-3   (of a quarterly)
              volume 8
              volume 10-12

        853   20   $6 1   $a v.   $b no.

        863   40   $6 1.1   $a 1-5   $w g

        863   40   $6 1.2   $a 7   $b 1-3   $w n

        863   40   $6 1.3   $a 8   $w g

        863   40   $6 1.4   $a 10-12

NISO display:  v.1-5,v.7:no.1-3;v.8,v.10-12
```

FIGURE 12

tuation required in the Z39.44 standard. A gap is designated by a comma; a nongap is designated by a semicolon.

Supplements/Accompanying Materials

A different set of tags is used to define fields of holdings data for supplements and accompanying materials. The 854 contains the Definition of Enumeration and Chronology/Publication Pattern for Supplements/Accompanying Material, just as the 853 contains that information for the basic bibliographic unit. The subfields of the 853 and 854 are nearly the same; the latter has an additional subfield noting the type of supplement or accompanying material.

Just as the 853 has its actual enumeration and chronology data in its companion 863, the 854 has a companion 864 containing the enumeration and chronology data for the supplement or accompanying material.

These unique tags are used to allow appropriate displays of this type material, separate from the basic bibliographic unit's holdings. Also, this type of material follows a different publication pattern than that of the basic bibliographic unit's holdings, and this must be recognized if this data is to be manipulated for displays.

Indexes

The same concept applies to indexes, which have a companion set of fields, the 855 and the 865 (Figure 13). Again, the subfields are basically the same as in the 853/863 sets of fields.

It is particularly important that the data representing indexes be identified separately since the compression of that data changes the meaning. For example, holdings where each volume represents a different year takes on a new meaning if compression implies a cumulation into a 10-year index. Therefore, the indicators which deal with compression differ from those in the 853/863 fields.

```
855/865 Fields for Indexes

        Vols. 1/5 (1936/1940)
        Vols. 6/10 (1941/1945)


           does not equal


        Vols. 1/10 (1936/1945)


    855    __ $6 1  $a v.  $o Author index  $i (year)

    865   41 $6 1.1  $a 1/5  $i 1936/1940

    865   41 $6 1.2  $a 6/10  $i 1941/1945


            Since this data cannot be compressed without
            changing its meaning, the 855 indicators are blank.
```

FIGURE 13

34 THE USMARC FORMAT FOR HOLDINGS AND LOCATIONS

Alternative Display Fields

Realizing the difficulty of formatting some very complex holdings statements, the format allows for a free-text notation of that data. Field 866 is used instead of the 853/863 fields to record all or part of the holdings.

The field may be used to record, in free text, holdings information which is recorded in the 853/863 fields. In that instance, the 866 may be used as an alternative display, ignoring the formatted data for display.

One likely use of the 866 is to transfer existing machine-readable records from older union list projects into 866 fields. This is basically a changing of the tag used for that data. A library could then decide to record all future holdings in 853/863 fields, if desired.

The 867 is an alternative display field for the accompanying material and supplement field tags, 854/864. The 868 is the alternative display for the 855/865 fields for indexes.

CONVERSION OF EXISTING MACHINE-READABLE RECORDS TO MARC

Given the amount of holdings and location data already available as machine-readable information in online catalogs, union lists, and other applications, the format was designed to insure flexibility for converting such data to the new MARC format.

It seems likely, for many of the existing non-MARC formats, that the location and call number information could be translated into the appropriate fields of the 852. Exact formatting of the call number might not be possible, but the call number can be contained in a single subfield, if necessary. In some cases, it will be possible to generate the classification type.

Depending upon the formatting of existing machine-readable records, it might be possible to transfer data elements into the subfields of the 853 and 863 fields. This, however, becomes more complicated for serials with complex publication patterns and if the holdings statements contain many gaps or breaks. It is less probable that the publication pattern information would be in the existing machine-readable record.

Most likely, many of the existing databases of holdings information will be loaded into the 866 field, the alternative display field, which is a free-text field. Captions as well as enumeration and chronology may all be included in that field.

In this approach, it is not necessary to know and store the publication pattern of that data. As free text, it could not be manipulated (or at least not easily or consistently). Future data entered into 853/863 and related fields could include publication pattern definitions. The indicators of the fields indicate the level of reporting and encoding of the information in the various fields.

While this is not a major consideration or problem within the format, it does potentially create some issues related to public displays of that data. The information entered in the 866 field will display exactly as entered. The library must then decide whether the data entered into the formatted fields (853/863) will be displayed in a similar manner, according to a level of the national standard (Z39.44), or according to a locally defined pattern. If a single system receives data from various sources of earlier machine-readable records, there may be inconsistencies of data in the different 866 fields. Obviously, the scenario could be carried further. A principle issue is to consider data display consistency in planning for machine-readable holdings data. A major advantage of the formatted data is that the display is flexible and can be changed in the future, just as systems handle bibliographic information now.

STATUS

The format is being used by various systems now, although the extent is still limited. Many automation vendors and local developments have followed the review and revising of the format as it evolved. Different systems plan to use varying amounts of the format, depending upon the application involved.

As part of the Southeastern ARL Serials Project, the SOLINET automation efforts implemented the format to support that regional database. The system can compress the holdings statements into detailed summary statements. Public displays of the data were generated according to the definitions of the Z39.44 standard, although

36 THE USMARC FORMAT FOR HOLDINGS AND LOCATIONS

a locally defined display was later adapted for the project. While that system did not address expansion of holdings to issue-by-issue statements, programmers have examined the structure and feel it is possible if all the data elements are supplied.

Many other systems have implemented some aspects of the format. These libraries and vendors have all provided comments and information to the MARBI Committee and the Library of Congress Network Development and MARC Standards Office. This information will be used in reviewing the format, leading to proposals for changing or enhancing the format. In this case, the process established for changing or enhancing the MARC bibliographic formats will be followed. Specifically, proposals will be reviewed by the MARBI Committee and the Library of Congress USMARC Advisory Group and the changes will be recommended to the Library of Congress.

The *USMARC Format for Holdings and Locations* was initially developed for serial holdings statements. Subsequently, it has been reviewed for its ability to handle all types of formats. Basically, it appears that the necessary fields for monographs exist. Complexities arise in considering music scores, multimedia kits, maps, and some other formats.

The NISO Z39 Subcommittee W is currently working to establish a standard for nonserial holdings. Once that work is completed, the *USMARC Format for Holdings and Locations* will be reviewed by MARBI and the library community. As with the bibliographic formats, the holdings format will evolve to support new developments in standards and practices relating to those types of data.

Reviews of the format to date anticipate that changes to handle additional formats will result in adding new fields and subfields. It is not expected that fields defined for serials would be redefined or changed so that data encoded for serial holdings would be invalid.

SUMMARY

The *USMARC Format for Holdings and Locations* appears to have achieved its goal of providing a format for the encoding of holdings and locations data. Thus encoded data then offers flexibility in display formats for both online and print products.

Use to date, while also raising some suggestions and proposals for enhancements, has shown that the format can be used to generate a variety of displays, including those defined by the levels of Z39.44, the standard for serial holdings displays. Libraries converting their holdings according to the format indicate that the learning and processing curve are not major problems. While the format appears complex, few records and applications seem to require many of the fields or subfields.

Undoubtedly the format will continue to evolve, as have the bibliographic and authorities MARC Formats. Given its inherent difference of allowing data manipulation rather than only display of information, this format also offers the potential of significant gains in collection management and resource sharing. Its implementation in existing and future automation systems will be a major issue in the next decade.

NOTES

1. Andrew D. Osborn, *Serial Publications: Their Place and Treatment in Libraries* (Chicago: American Library Association, 1980), pp. 24-48.

2. *USMARC Format for Holdings and Locations*, Final Draft (Washington, Library of Congress, 1984).

3. "The USMARC Format: Underlying Principles," *Library of Congress Information Bulletin* 42 (May 9, 1983): 148-152.

4. For additional information and background on the development of the format, see also: Linda H. Sapp, "The USMARC Format for Holdings and Locations," *Drexel Library Quarterly* 21 (1985): 87-100.

5. The original participating institutions were Emory University, University of Florida, Florida State University, University of Georgia, University of Kentucky, University of Miami, University of Tennessee, and Virginia Polytechnic Institute and State University.

6. American National Standards Institute, *American National Standard for Information Sciences—Serial Holdings Statements* (New York: ANSI, 1986). (ANSI Z39.44-1986).

7. In July 1986, the ALA MARBI Committee approved a proposal to add an 852 $x and an 863 $x as additional note subfields. With this revision $x is defined as a nonpublic note; $z is a public note for general display with the holdings information.

38   THE USMARC FORMAT FOR HOLDINGS AND LOCATIONS

8. All figures showing examples of formatted data have spaces inserted between elements to facilitate readability. These spaces are not part of the format.

9. In January 1987, the ALA MARBI Committee discussed removing preservation information from the 863 field and creating a new separate field for various types of preservation information. Further discussion at future MARBI meetings may approve this change.

SOLINET's Implementation of the *USMARC Format for Holdings and Locations*

Michele I. Dalehite

The new *USMARC Format for Holdings and Locations* is the latest in a series of standards to control library data that has been developed via cooperative action by individuals, institutions, and organizations. The history of that development has been documented elsewhere in this volume. SOLINET's (Southeastern Library Network) opportunity to be a part of this "birth of a format" as it were began in the fall of 1983. The directors of the Southeastern ARL (SEARL) libraries who were participating in a serials conversion project, funded by an Office of Education Title II-C Grant, approached SOLINET with a proposal. They wanted an independent organization to test the feasibility of this newly developing format. Most particularly, they wanted to be certain that the format would work as a mechanism for recording serial holdings in a structure that would enable the data to be manipulated: specifically, that the detailed holdings data could be edited for both errors in format integrity and data content; that it could be compressed into a condensed form; and finally, that it could be formatted into a display that conformed to the NISO standards for displaying serial holdings.

SOLINET subcontracted with the Burroughs Corporation for the technical expertise needed to conduct an analysis and produce a feasibility report. Burroughs had completed a number of develop-

---

Michele I. Dalehite is Assistant Director for Program Development, The Florida Center for Library Automation.

40   THE USMARC FORMAT FOR HOLDINGS AND LOCATIONS

ment projects for SOLINET and could be relied upon to produce a result that would satisfy both SOLINET and the SEARL libraries.

During the winter of 1983 and spring of 1984, the Burroughs development team worked on a document known as pseudocode, a program-like document which could be used by anyone who wished to write software to perform three basic functions: EDIT, COMPRESS, and DISPLAY. The pseudocode was written in ALGOL which is the Burroughs standard higher level language for large systems.

The pseudocode was reviewed by programmers at the University of Georgia, Harvard University, the Library of Congress, and other interested parties. In late spring it was accepted by the SEARL directors and Phase II began. In Phase II, the SEARL libraries wanted a working model which demonstrated the three primary functions against holdings records which conformed to the format standards:

- the ability to initiate an error-detection command which would flag all syntax and content errors,
- the ability to perform a compression command resulting in multiple holdings statements being condensed into the most compact string possible, and
- the ability to produce a display of the data that conformed to NISO standards for serial holdings.

In the spring of 1984, Burroughs produced this working model, it was reviewed by representatives from both SOLINET and SEARL, and was judged to adequately demonstrate the ability to EDIT, COMPRESS, and DISPLAY serial holdings data. Once a working model existed, the SEARL directors came back to SOLINET with a request that a fully operational online system be developed which would allow the SEARL libraries to build databases of serial holdings records in the new *USMARC Format for Holdings and Locations*.

SOLINET and Burroughs management negotiated a contract which called for the implementation of such a system. A development team composed of SOLINET systems and member services staff and Burroughs programmer/analysts was formulated. A number of significant issues had to be resolved at the beginning:

Would this newly emerging system need to function as a serials control subsystem? Not immediately, was the SEARL response; it was not in the scope of the SEARL grant to test the new format for that function.

Would this new system have to be completely independent of the existing SOLINET Online System which had been created from the conversion of the WLN software (known as LAMBDA)? There was considerable discussion of this issue. SOLINET wanted to be able to take advantage of all of the retrieval capabilities that LAMBDA offered for bibliographic records (keyword, boolean, subject search, etc.). Also, it was felt that the existence of a serial holdings subsystem for the SOLINET Online System would be a desirable feature. The SEARL directors were concerned that their project might be subsumed under the larger set of services encompassed by LAMBDA and therefore would not get the attention needed. In addition, there were concerns that if the serials system developed by SOLINET was not independent, other libraries would be able to create holdings of their own and access holdings of the SEARL libraries, thereby benefitting from a project designed and funded for ARL libraries. After considerable debate, it was decided that SOLINET's resources were not sufficient to accommodate two completely independent online systems and that it would be in the long-term best interests of the SEARL libraries if SOLINET had such a new service that could be available to current and prospective LAMBDA users.

Would this new subsystem be used for just serial holdings, leaving the old holdings subsystem in place for nonserial items? There was strong opposition to having two very different holdings subsystems on LAMBDA; it would be confusing for both staff and patrons. The existing holdings subsystem had been developed by SOLINET; it was not the WLN version. While it provided for storing, editing, and displaying location and call number data, it did not adequately handle copy and volume data for either monographs or serials. An analysis of the *USMARC Format for Holdings and Locations* indicated that it would be feasible to adapt it to monographic

42 THE USMARC FORMAT FOR HOLDINGS AND LOCATIONS

holdings, although there were no NISO standards in place yet to provide guidance for displays and it did not address the unique needs of nonprint materials.

LAMBDA STRUCTURE AND THE HOLDINGS FORMAT

The SOLINET Online System provided an amenable environment for the new holdings format. A resource (or union) bibliographic file containing all of the unique records used by any of the LAMBDA users (current or former) was the primary file in the database. This file was designed to allow partitioning by institution to enable either separate storage of full bibliographic records (redundant to the resource record but containing variances) or storage of index links to the resource record. In either case, the subset of records for each institution could be searched independently of the resource file. The bibliographic file was designed to store the data applicable to the description of published works regardless of which institution owned them. No local notes, location, or call number data were to be stored in the bibliographic record. With this design, it was easier for libraries to share the resource bibliographic record and the responsibility for maintaining it.

Each authoritative heading in the bibliographic records was linked to a corresponding record in the authority file which could also be partitioned by institution if local authorities were desired. The working file provided a temporary storage facility for bibliographic and authority records in the process of being input or changed. This feature allowed the process to be interrupted indefinitely or enabled records to be reviewed by other staff members before they went through the overnight indexing procedures.

A third file, the detailed holdings file, also was partitioned by institution. Since holdings data, by its nature, would have no data common to the resource database, the partitions were only for individual institutions. The detailed holdings records were linked to the bibliographic records by the Record Identifier (RID) which was usually the OCLC number. A third storage option, exercised by the SEARL libraries, allowed holdings records to link directly to resource bibliographic records, thereby reducing the storage costs. With the separation of bibliographic and holdings data already a

Michele I. Dalehite 43

feature of the SOLINET system, replacing the existing holdings subsystem with a new version based on the *USMARC Format for Holdings and Locations* was a feasible objective for the design team to undertake.

HOLDINGS FORMAT IMPLEMENTATION

Before work began on the holdings format implementation, several changes were made to the original LAMBDA system. The most significant change, required to support an increased activity in searching of serial titles, was the creation of a straight title index. Prior to this project, the only title access was to the main title/ subtitle (i.e., 245 field) by keyword and implicit boolean. This was most beneficial for finding titles by a few known words or by subtitle words, but it did pose a problem for searching many serial titles where the words are not very explicit, such as *TIME* or *Journal of American History*. To aid the users of the system in retrieving the serial titles they would need for holdings work, the entire database was re-indexed to create a separate title index called a Linear Title Index which used the title in exact order rather than individual words. With this index, users could search titles two different ways, choosing the method that would work best for any given serial. In addition, the new index could be browsed forward and backward so the user could enter just the first few words of a title and retrieve a list of titles from which to choose. Additional title fields were indexed in the new index to expand access to variant titles.

One problem not fully anticipated when the project began quickly revealed itself once work on the format commenced: there was no authority to turn to for interpretation of the format documentation. A number of times the format design team was asked for a ruling on an apparent contradiction only to have the team itself not be able to agree on what its intent had been. The MARBI committee (the ALA committee responsible for reviewing and approving all MARC formats) had added and changed elements of the format during one of its passes by that group. The committee members were not readily available to answer questions. It was obvious that some of the additions had been made without real assurance that they did not conflict with other parts of the format. A very real confusion over how

44 *THE USMARC FORMAT FOR HOLDINGS AND LOCATIONS*

copy numbers should be handled seems to have grown out of a last minute revision that is illustrated in the conflict in the description of usage of subfield t in the 852 and 863 fields. Each referred to the other, leaving the reader in doubt as to whether it was ever appropriate to use subfield t. Both were unclear as to how subfield t copy information was to conform to the number of copies element in the 008 field bytes 17-19. The SOLINET team had to make an interpretation of the copy subfields based on the practical needs of its users. Essentially, use of 863 subfield t was prohibited because each individual holdings record was to represent a single copy unless the record was a composite record, in which case no copy members were to be recorded in the holdings fields at all. Instead, the number of copies reflected in the record would be entered in the 008/17-19.

Some of the other interpretations and local decisions which had to be made were:

LEADER: The bibliographic level from the leader of the bibliographic record to which the holdings record was attached was moved to the Bibliographic Level position of the holdings record. While the holdings format leaves it blank, its presence would be needed to be able to extract or count the holdings records for serials and monographs without having to retrieve the bibliographic record.

LANG: The bibliographic record language code was automatically supplied on the workform for a new record but the operator could change it. In the SOLINET system it is not used to generate the captions, however, since only the English language captions are in the conversion tables. No standards for month and season names exist in all other languages and none had been agreed upon by the SEARL committee at the time of system implementation.

852 FIELD: Second indicator values of 8 and 9 to identify call numbers from 098 and 099 fields were added; the original 098 and 099 indicators were stored in a

new subfield 8. These changes were needed to preserve the original call number data from OCLC transaction records. Subfields p and t for item numbers and copy numbers were made repeatable for single volume monographs so that there would not have to be a separate 852 field for every copy. This decision saved storage and manual input and edit time. If the subfield t did not contain alphas (i.e., caption data) the system supplied ''c.'' in the displays of that data.

85X &
86X FIELDS: Subfield x for nondisplaying notes was added after the system was implemented because the users found many instances when they wanted to record a note about a particular piece or the whole title that they did not want to display to the public. The format did not have such a feature.

When the decision was made to replace the old holding subsystem with the new one, the design team not only had the challenge of designing this new creature, but also of determining how the existing online holdings data would be converted into the new format. It was very quickly decided that since this conversion would be a one-time process, the existing data would be converted back to the OCLC 049 and call number fields from which it was originally derived. Then a new dataload program would be written for the conversion of OCLC 049 data to the new MARC format. This conversion program would be needed indefinitely. Once the existing data was converted back to the original OCLC format, this newly created data was run through the new standard load format software. Care had to be taken to insure that the data was not corrupted during either of the processes. The other problem faced was that during the time the new holdings subsystem was being implemented and the old one was being abandoned, no new data could be loaded and the libraries could not modify any of their online holdings data. This process took about 1 full month to complete. Eleven LAMBDA users and about 15 retrospective conversion projects were affected by this major revision of the database. Approximately two and a half million holdings records were converted. There were

46 THE USMARC FORMAT FOR HOLDINGS AND LOCATIONS

significant retraining requirements for all of the existing LAMBDA users and the recon staff as well as the new training for the SEARL library staff members who would be using LAMBDA and the *US-MARC Format for Holdings and Locations* for the first time.

The product of that conversion effort is illustrated in Figure 1. Since the old holdings format contained only location, call number, and local note data, the new MARC records constructed from this data were limited to the LEADER, 008, and 852 fields. Default values were supplied for the LEADER and 008 field based on the type of bibliographic record to which the holdings were linked.

Not long into the design stage, the issue of storage requirements for MARC holdings records became a strong concern of the team. While the implementation of the new format might be viewed as an exercise in testing its theoretical possibilities, the team was fully cognizant of the potential impact on storage this new format would have if a literal interpretation was made. The particular problem area was in the requirement that every variance in location/call number must be recorded in a separate record. While this requirement addressed the communications format rather than the internal storage format, any design allowing more compact storage had to accommodate output of the data in the communications format.

Single volume monographs were seen to be the problem area. Public library users of LAMBDA frequently had dozens if not hundreds of copies of a given title located in a number of collections or branches. To put each of these in a separate MARC record would require the overhead of LEADER and 008 data which would have a high probability of being identical. A more compact structure which would reduce storage requirements was seen to be imperative. To accommodate this need, a record structure allowing multiple occurrences of the 852 field was developed. This structure would be valid only when the LEADER type was "x" and bibliographic level was "m." Other local fields from the institution's OCLC tape record could be stored in this record as well; fields such as 049, 590, 910, and 949. Figure 1 illustrates a single volume monographic holdings record.

A new dilemma faced the design team; the new MARC holdings format not only allowed but required multiple records to describe each physical location of a run of holdings for a given serials title.

OLD FORMAT

```
DHF  R  290058/FMMAINFM/L    aPZ$c.M6984$dGo
DHF  R  290058/SPMAINSM/L    aPS3525$c.I972$eG6$f1938
DHF  R  290058/TPMAINMM/L    aPA3525$c.I972$eG6
        DH01 049     $aFHFM
        DH02 049     $aFHSM
        DH03 049     $aFHMM$c1-2
```

NEW FORMAT

```
dhf r 290058
Mitchell, Margaret, 1900-1949.  * Gone with the wind      1936
HID:  290058-0000  Status: n   Entered: 841022   Updated:841022
         Type       BibLvl   EncLvl   R/AcqSt   MthAcq   Cancel   GenRet
  DHFX   [x]        [m]      [2]      [2]       [p]      [   ]    [8]
         [   ]      [4]      [004]    [a]       .[u]     [eng]    [0]
         SpeRet     Cmpl     Copy     Lend      Repro    Lang     C/SInd
  DHO0001 852 0     $bFHFM$hPZ3$i.M6984 Go
  DHO0002 852 0     $bFHMM$hPS3525.I972$iG6 1936$t1-2
  DHO0003 852 0     $bFHMS$hPS3525.I972$iG6
```

FIGURE 1. Holdings Records, Old and New Formats

48 THE USMARC FORMAT FOR HOLDINGS AND LOCATIONS

This could mean separate subscriptions (i.e., copies) or split runs housed in two locations. Regardless of frequency of occurrence, every library would have some titles which would require multiple logical records that had to be linked to a single bibliographic record. The solution devised by the SOLINET team was to create two levels of records. The first level called the CONTROL record linked to the bibliographic record and served as a directory to the second level or EXTENT records. The CONTROL record also provided a convenient place to put local OCLC tape fields (e.g., 049, 590, 910, and 949) that did not belong anywhere else. The EXTENT records contained the actual MARC holdings data elements; LEADER, 008, 852, 853, 863, and so forth. As with the holdings records for single volume monographs, the Record Identifier (RID) linked the bibliographic records to the holdings records. The Holdings Identifier (HID) was composed of the RID followed by a four digit suffix. The CONTROL record suffix was always -0000. Each EXTENT record was assigned the next available number beginning with -0001. The suffix could increase to -8999. Numbers -9000 to -9999 were reserved for records in the process of being input. Once stored permanently in the database, a permanent suffix would be assigned. Figure 2 illustrates the CONTROL record and one EXTENT record for the title *Library Journal*.

As was previously mentioned, the CONTROL record served as a directory to the individual EXTENT records. This was made possible by the presence of system-created 866 fields which contained the display version of the holdings data. Included in that field were the HID, location data, call number, status data area, notes, and extent of holdings. Although the presence of these fields required duplicate storage, the benefits in improved response time in producing public catalog and union list displays made it justifiable. The 866 fields had a second indicator of 9 to distinguish them from user input 866 fields. These system-created fields could not be accessed or modified online. The need to store duplicate data applied only to multi-volume monographs and to serials; the majority of records in the database were single-volume monographs. SOLINET does make the system-created 866 fields available on the MARC output tapes if requested. Users who may not be able to produce a display version of the MARC data initially find them to be useful. While

CONTROL

```
dhf r 2351916                                        DH INQUIRY CONTROL
Library journal                                        v. 101   1976
HID:  2351916-0000   Status:  n      Entered:  841022  Updated:  850122
---------------------------------------------------------------------
2.   2351916-0001    EMLP
3.   2351916-0002    EMOP
```

EXTENT

```
s 2                                                   DH INQUIRY EXTENT
Library Journal                                         v. 101   1976
HID:  2351916-001    Status:  n     Entered:  841022   Updated:  850122
     Type     BibLvl   EncLvl   R/AcqSt  MthAcq   Cancel   GenRet
DHFX [y]      [s]      [2]      [2]      [p]      [ ]      [8]
     [ ]      [0]      [001]    [a]      [a]      [eng]    [0]
     SpeRet   Cmpl     Copy     Lend     Repro    Lang     C/SInd
DH0001 852    $bEMLP
DH0002 853    11$61$av.$i(year)
DH0003 863    40$61.1$a101-:09$i1976-1984
```

FIGURE 2. CONTROL and EXTENT Records

50 THE USMARC FORMAT FOR HOLDINGS AND LOCATIONS

some manipulation is required, the meshing of caption and enumeration text and the insertion of punctuation have already been supplied.

It was mentioned earlier that there was no resource level holdings data, but initially in the implementation of the new holdings subsystem, this was not the case. Very early on, the design team proposed the creation of a resource level record intended to store publication pattern data which could be shared by all. Called "model" records, these very minimal records would be created from the 853/4/5 fields found in the first EXTENT record stored for a given serial. Each time an input workform was requested, the 853/4/5 data would be inserted to serve as a template. The concept was worthwhile, but the implementation proved to be unsatisfactory. The quality of the 85X fields in the model records was consistently low since frequently the first record input contained errors or, at best, was an incomplete history of the publication's patterns. In addition, use of subfield 3 for the definition date span was never established as an input standard by the SEARL libraries so subsequent users could not readily use the 853/4/5 fields without researching the pattern history again. Finally, there was no evidence of a strong interest in sharing the responsibility for maintaining the model records. Given all of these drawbacks, shortly after system implementation the model records were deleted and the software was modified to eliminate the procedure which created them.

A new feature added at about the same time that the model records were deleted helped compensate for the loss of this function. It was quickly determined by the users that holdings conversion could be greatly facilitated by an ability to copy an EXTENT record either within the same institution (as in a first copy) or from another institution. Considerable keying could be eliminated if the run of holdings were identical or even similar. In response to this need, a COPY command was implemented. The operator could identify the source record (RID and institution) to be copied and the destination (i.e., the bibliographic record to which the new holdings record should be linked). All local text would be deleted, such as location codes and nondisplaying notes.

Prior to the training of the SEARL staff members and the beginning of the serial holdings input, SOLINET initiated two data loading projects to assist the SEARL libraries with their holdings conversion projects. The first dataload project called for the selection of all serials bibliographic records from each library's OCLC transaction files. The duplicate records were eliminated for each library and the records were loaded into the SOLINET Online System. Any new bibliographic records not found in the resource file were added. The 049 data and corresponding call numbers were extracted from all of the records and formed into a brief MARC format record which contained an 008 field and an 852 field. These brief (or, as they were called, skeletal) records served as workforms for the input of the MARC holdings. The second load was of CONSER and LC Serials records to upgrade the bibliographic file and to expand its scope as more libraries began holdings conversion projects. These records were loaded into the resource bibliographic file. This load was not complete when the SEARL libraries began the data entry, but the first load supplied all of the records that they needed.

EDIT, CONTROL, DISPLAY

With the preliminaries resolved, the three major functions remain to be described. Although each of these functions was specified and coded in both the original pseudocode and the working model, they underwent several iterations during the initial development phase and again in a major revision made in the spring of 1985 following a review by the SEARL advisory committee. The EDIT function proved to be quite complex to implement. There were two editorial requirements: 1) the integrity of the MARC structure, tags, indicator, subfield codes; and 2) the content of the data elements.

The first requirement was relatively easy to meet: a table was built which listed which tags are valid for the format and which indicators and subfields are valid for each tag. The complexity increases when certain tags, indicators, and subfields are valid only on a conditional basis. For example, the ENC LVL in the leader identifies what the specificity of holdings is as defined by NISO (i.e., how detailed). Depending upon the value recorded, some tags may not be allowed in the record. For example, at level 2, neither 853/4/5 or 863/4/5/6 field groups can be input.

In the online display, errors in the fixed field were highlighted in

52 THE USMARC FORMAT FOR HOLDINGS AND LOCATIONS

reverse video. Errors in the variable field were highlighted by an error code in the left margin of the screen, also in reverse video. Very early in the development of the SOLINET Online System, the commitment was made to support the OCLC terminals currently in use: models 100, 105, and M300. As such, line by line transmission of fields was required since these terminals have no forms mode for full screen transmission. Errors were not highlighted until the EDIT command was entered. At that time, the entire contents of the record was edited. This requirement was primarily because many errors could not be detected until the entire record was created. While a field may be technically accurate by itself, it may not be accurate in conjunction with another field in the record. There is a considerable amount of interaction between fields in the holding format, particularly between the 85X and 86X fields.

Since SOLINET was commissioned to thoroughly test the EDIT function, it implemented considerable editing features. Others who have programmed for this format have not gone to such lengths and have been able to develop a system faster. Forty-two error codes and 40 error messages inform the user of error conditions that range from the general (Editing errors exist) to the specific (DEC-code identifying that the decimal point in an 863/4/5 field is missing). Some other error codes and their meanings are:

COM CANNOT BE COMPRESSED-insufficient coding in 853/ 4/5

DPF DUPLICATE FIELD ($6 VALUE)-multiple 853/4/5 fields with the same $6 contents

DTO COMPRESS FOUND DATA OVERLAP-compression resulted in an overlap of holdings in 863/4/5/ fields

FOR FIELD ORDER-$6 values are duplicated or nonascending

GAP 863/4/5 $w MUST BE g OR n

SFC SUBFIELD CONTENTS-not accurate in the context of this field and/or record

SUM SUMMARY NOT LAST-863/4/5 field ends in hyphen but is not the last occurrence in record

Michele I. Dalehite 53

Despite the sophistication of the editing software, much of the burden for data integrity falls on the user, however, since accuracy in publication patterns and holdings content depend on correct interpretation of the format documentation and the sources of holdings data (e.g., KARDEX files, shelflists, printouts, etc.).

One of the editing errors that the system highlights is identified when the system attempts to compress the data to produce the display. As mentioned previously, to increase efficiency of retrieval and improve response time, each time a holdings record is modified and restored in the database, a new display image of that data is created and stored in an 866 field in the CONTROL record. When an EXTENT record is attempted to be restored into the database, the system automatically compresses the holdings (if the 853 is coded as being compressible). The point of doing this is to produce a more compact text string for the end user. What might be keyed into 10 separate fields in the record may compress into two lines of text in the patron display. If there is any data integrity error that prevents compression from working, then an error message is returned. The error must be resolved before the record can be accepted by the system.

Another feature of the system is the working file, a place where records in the process of being input or edited can be stored temporarily. Modeled after the original working file for bibliographic and authority records, this file is handy if there is a need for a supervisor to review an operator's work or, for some reason, completion of the work on a record is delayed. The file is in the library's control and the records stay in the working file until taken out by the library staff. Also, there is a protection against multiple users of one record. Any number of users can view one MARC format holdings record, but only one can work on it at a time. The first user to enter the change command gets it and all others are locked out of anything but viewing it. This is true even if the record is stored in the working file.

It must be emphasized that automatic compression only affects the holdings display, the actual MARC record is unchanged. There is an explicit COMPRESS command however, that when used will actually reduce the number of 86X fields in the record to the fewest that it can. Although this feature was included in the SEARL specifications, it has not been used other than for testing. The general

54 THE USMARC FORMAT FOR HOLDINGS AND LOCATIONS

consensus of practice was to input the data in as detailed or compressed form as desired for permanent storage. The major benefit for an explicit COMPRESS capability would be to initiate the compression of individual issues to the volume level as might be required in a check-in function.

The COMPRESS function, whether initiated by the user or performed by the system to create the display form of the data, is accomplished by analyzing the 853/4/5 fields for all of the data elements required for compression to work. Once the pattern has been established, the corresponding 863/4/5 fields are analyzed to determine if the enumeration is in ascending order. In essence, the software predicts the next logical value in the enumeration subfields, then tests the next field for its presence. If the value found is incompatible, then a gap break is assumed. If the value is compatible but the second indicator is set to 4, then a nongap break is assumed. Appropriate punctuation is supplied. No testing of chronology is performed; the contents of the chronology subfields are simply carried along with the enumeration. Early testing of the format uncovered too many inconsistencies between enumeration and chronology (primarily for law materials) to enable consistent compression (i.e., prediction) of both.

It was very difficult to program for compression of some publication patterns. When the chronology was recorded as primary enumeration and the frequency was greater than monthly, any irregularity in the publication pattern made prediction of the expected contents of contiguous 863 fields to determine whether a gap existed virtually impossible. Use of the generic "(date)" value in the subfield a guaranteed the data would be noncompressible since no regular pattern could be established. Also, the use of season codes was problematic since there are no standards for determining what the first season of a year is. The format assigns the values 21 to spring, 22 to summer, 23 to fall, and 24 to winter, but a publication may change volumes with the winter issue resulting in a sequence of season codes as follows: 24, 21, 22, 23. In the SOLINET system, the year would have to be entered with a slash (i.e., 1984/1985) to indicate that the volume spanned two years. Many hours of discussion took place before the design team reconciled itself to the fact that not every record was going to be compressible even if the publication pattern was regular. For example, it was determined that 853 fields with c, i, j, or s in the subfield w could not be coded as being compressible because there would be no way to predict incrementation.

Besides the *USMARC Format for Holdings and Locations*, a second national standard was integral to this project: the *American National Standard For Information Science – Serials Holdings Statements* (Z39.44) – frequently referred to as the NISO standard. In the original specifications from the SEARL group, they wanted the public displays to conform to NISO. After the system was brought up in fall of 1984, the SEARL advisory committee was not totally happy with the public displays, particularly for the level 4 detailed holdings. NISO calls for a pattern of enumeration and chronology that interleaves the two for each unbroken range. Figure 3 illustrates the NISO Standard for a complex range of holdings data. For many of the committee members, this display resulted in some visual con-

```
DETAILED HOLDINGS DATA

    863  ....  $a 1-10 $g 1-60 $i 1961-1970
    863  ....  $a 11 $b 1-3 $g 61-63 $i 1971 $j 01-06
    863  ....  $a 12-20 $g 67-120 $i 1972-1980
    863  ....  $a 21 $b 2-6 $g 122-126 $i 1981 $j 03-12
    863  ....  $a 22-25 $g 127-150 $i 1982-1985
```

```
NISO DISPLAY

    v.1=no.1 (1961)-v.10=no.60 (1970) v.11:pt.1=no.61
    (1971:Jan)-v.11:pt.3=no.63 (1971:June), v.12=no.67
    (1972)-v.20=no.120 (1980), v.21:pt.2=no.122 (1981:
    March)-v.21:pt.6=no.126 (1981;Dec.) v.22=no.127
    (1982)-v.25=no.150 (1985)
```

```
SOLINET DISPLAY

    v.1-v.10=no.1-no.60 (1961-1970)
    v.11:pt.1-v.11:pt.3=no.61-no.63 (1971:Jan.-1971:June),
    v.12-v.20=no.67-no.120 (1972-1980),
    v.21:pt.2-v.21:pt.6=no.122-no.126 (1981:Mar.-1981:Dec.)
    v.22-v.25=no.127-no.150 (1982-1985)
```

FIGURE 3. Comparison of NISO and SOLINET Displays

fusion when there were variables such as gaps and alternate enumeration.

The committee requested that SOLINET modify the displays to be more like option 2 of level 3 in the NISO standard. This option (not normally available for level 4) allows for creating complete ranges of enumeration and chronology until each gap. The committee felt that this would produce a more readable display for the public. Figure 3 also illustrates the revised version of the display. Other changes in spacing, indentions, and order of data were recommended as well. The revised specifications required more than a rewriting of the software that generated the display format. Since the display data is actually stored in the database, once the software was rewritten, every multi-volume holdings record had to have its display fields regenerated. While not as difficult as the initial database conversion, it required over a week to reconstruct the display data according to the new specifications.

There are other features of the public display besides the formatting of the actual volumes and dates. Certain coded data in the fixed fields are actually converted to text strings to provide additional information for the user. It was the intent of the format designers that this content could be stored efficiently in a coded form and could also provide the flexibility of changes in wording without rekeying the text. Only a table of literal phrases linked to the codes has to be changed.

It is important to note that the decision to deviate from the NISO standards for the display did not affect the format of the holdings data itself; it is still stored in the record as required by the US-MARC format regardless of how it is displayed. This is one of the benefits of having this standard input format; the data is shareable, but the way it is displayed is variable.

Figures 2, 4, and 5 illustrate the variety of displays of the same record possible in the SOLINET system. Figure 2 shows the version of the record normally seen by the technical services personnel responsible for its maintenance. Using the RID to retrieve the record, the user is presented with the CONTROL record display which contains unmodifiable data above the hyphens such as bibliographic identification data (line 2), the Holdings Identifier of the CONTROL record, and LEADER data. The directory to the attached EXTENT records is listed below the line of hyphens. A selection of item number 2 results in the EXTENT record for the copy in EMLP. The modifiable data is identified by a line number beginning with the letters "DH." Note that the 852 begins with the subfield b. Subfield a is reserved for the institution identifier (NUC symbol). Subfield a is not stored in the online record, but it is supplied on the tape records.

Figure 4 illustrates the public catalog display of bibliographic and holdings data. Location codes convert to names and fixed field codes convert to text strings. Not all of the NISO status elements are reflected in the public catalog display. The two union displays provided by the system are illustrated in Figure 5. A search of the union bibliographic file produces a display which summarizes the institutions which have holdings attached to this bibliographic item. The NUC symbols are sorted alphabetically. Selection of an institution results in a display somewhat similar to Figure 4 but it follows the NISO standard for coded status data area. The institution is identified by the NUC symbol. The locations are still coded also. SOLINET developed a COM union serials list product that can merge holdings from multiple institutions and attach them to a single bibliographic record. The COM display of the holdings data is very similar to the online display illustrated in the second part of Figure 5.

CONCLUSION

The cooperative development project undertaken by SOLINET and the SEARL libraries produced a functional and well-received tool that aided both organizations in accomplishing their respective objectives. The SEARL libraries were able to test their new holdings format in a sophisticated, interactive online environment. Several of the libraries were able to create considerable databases of MARC holdings records which will provide the flexibility and mobility that are associated with MARC data.

SOLINET was able to add an attractive and highly desirable component to its online services. Just as important, the organization had an opportunity to be a leader in both a regional and, in time, national movement as the new format moved beyond the SEARL group that designed it and officially became part of the MARC family and entered the consciousness of the larger library community.

```
f 1 76-645271                                          BIB FULL DISPLAY
     Library journal. -- [New York, Bowker].
     v. ill. 29 cm. semimonthly (monthly, July-Aug.).
     Continues:  LJ, Library journal.
     Keytitle:  Library journal (1976).  ISSN: 0363-0277 0000-0027.
     1. Library science--Periodicals.  2. Libraries--United States.
     NSD NSD DLC NSD OCL NSD FQG.  LCCN:  76645271.  RID:  2351916.


     Location(s), Call Number(s), Extent of Holdings

         Library Science    Currently received.
          v.101-v.109  (1976-1984)
          Earlier vol. on microfiche.
         Oxford Periodicals Currently received.  Library
          retains latest 6 months.
```

FIGURE 4. Public Access Display

SUMMARY

```
 h iss 0363-0277                            UNION SUMMARY DISPLAY
 Library journal                                v.99        1974
 RID: 2351916         LCCN: 76645271         ISSN: 0363-0277


    1.  FU             3.  Nc
    2.  GEU            4.  TCollSM
```

DETAILED

```
 s 2                                        UNION DETAILED DISPLAY
 Library journal                                v. 101    1976
 RID:  2351916        LCCN:  76645271        ISSN:  0363-0277

 GEU   EMLS (850122,b,ta,1,5,8)  Currently received.
       v.101-v.109 (1976-1984)
       Earlier vol. on microfiche.
 GEU   EMOP (820523,b,ta,1,5,8)  Currently received.
       Library retains latest 6 months.
```

FIGURE 5. Union Summary and Detailed Display

Implementation of the
USMARC Format for
Holdings and Locations
at the Harvard University Library

Priscilla L. Caplan

The Harvard University Library is actually a decentralized system of nearly 100 libraries. They range in size from the main research library, with well over 3 million volumes, to small departmental collections counted in the hundreds. They are geographically dispersed among nine cities, four states, and two countries. The governance structure is complex, with administrative and fiscal responsibility for the units divided among nine Harvard faculties and a variety of affiliated museums, institutions, and research centers.

Not surprisingly, the various libraries comprising the University Library differ greatly in their policies, strengths, needs, services, philosophies, and priorities. More surprisingly, the last decade has seen ever-increasing cooperation between the units in the areas of collection development, preservation, and automated systems. Led by a succession of farsighted directors, the University Library has overseen the development of two major centralized processing systems. The Union Catalog Production System, implemented in 1981, produces a microfiche Union Catalog of the holdings of more than 70 contributing libraries. HOLLIS, the Harvard Online Library Information System, began operation for acquisitions and serials

---

Priscilla L. Caplan is Head, Systems Development Division, Office for Systems Planning and Research, Harvard University Library.

62 THE USMARC FORMAT FOR HOLDINGS AND LOCATIONS

control in July 1985, with the voluntary participation of 32 units. As a startled *LJ/SLJ hotline* announced to the world: "Harvard Plans for Cooperation with Itself"![1]

But Harvard cooperates with more than itself, particularly in the area of shared cataloging. The Library was an early participant in the national CONSER project, and has contributed or enhanced bibliographic records for approximately 30,000 serials since 1976. It was a charter member of NACO, and, along with the University of Chicago, one of the first two libraries to participate in the prototype LC Cooperative Cataloging Project, in which original cataloging is contributed directly to the Library of Congress for redistribution. Although the Library has long had the ability to create and maintain MARC records in-house, contributing locational information and shareable cataloging to the bibliographic utilities is considered an institutional obligation. Most Harvard University Library units belong to OCLC, and the Law, Fine Arts, and Loeb Music libraries catalog in RLIN through special memberships in RLG.

Before HOLLIS, the Library built and maintained holdings records for its CONSER serials in-house in a file called the HUL Holdings File. These records reported notes, captions, enumeration, and chronology using locally defined, MARC-like content designation. A batch processing system combined bibliographic data from CONSER serials and holdings data from the HUL Holdings File for display in the Union Catalog. When plans for HOLLIS were announced in 1982, the decision was made to store all serials and serial holdings information in the new online system. Since a conversion from the old HUL Holdings File format to a new record structure suitable for HOLLIS would be necessary in any case, the Library decided to review and perhaps redesign its internal holdings format.

At this time the *USMARC Format for Holdings and Locations* was still in early draft status, and the *American National Standard for Serial Holdings Statements at the Detailed Level* was a draft standard of the ANSI Z39 Subcommittee E. Both of these were in a somewhat fluid state, and it was far from clear whether, when complete, they would be compatible with each other or with the standard for serial holdings statements at the summary level (ANSI Standard Z39.42 1980). Nonetheless, there was a strong administrative concern that Harvard's holdings information be shareable with the widest number of other institutions; the University Library was no longer willing to support nonstandard holdings reporting.

At this point three alternatives were considered: to define the HOLLIS holdings record as a series of free text note fields into which holdings could be entered using ANSI notation; to modify the old HUL Holdings File format in such a way that an ANSI standard display could be easily derived; or to adopt the draft *US-MARC Format for Holdings and Locations*.

The second alternative was quickly rejected on the grounds that if data were to be content designated in any detailed way, a national MARC format should be preferred over yet another locally defined, MARC-like record. The issue became one of the relative merits of free text strings vs. a more highly encoded notation. Text strings would be easier for staff to enter and interpret, resulting in lower project costs in the short term, and reduced operational expenses over time. Also, less manipulation would be required for display in the Union Catalog and the future online catalog.

However, there were also strong arguments in favor of US-MARC. The ANSI recommendations for summary and detailed holdings have since been combined into a single unified standard, but at the time they were separate and not entirely compatible. There was some concern that a summary statement could not be derived by program from a detailed one, and that consequently either or both of the standards might undergo revision. The prospect of creating large numbers of holdings records in a notation that might soon become obsolete was not encouraging. This particular issue highlighted a major disadvantage of the free text field approach. When data is entered as text strings it is basically inert, and can only be reformatted with extensive textual analysis. On the other hand, when the elements comprising a holdings statement are clearly tagged and delimited, different display formats can be generated for different purposes, or as display conventions change over time.

Similarly, it was understood that more highly content-designated data has more potential utility. Although relatively sophisticated functions such as automatic compression of item-by-item reports or prediction of next expected issue were not planned for the initial

64 THE USMARC FORMAT FOR HOLDINGS AND LOCATIONS

implementation of HOLLIS, the Library did not want to preclude such development in the future. The University Library views its machine-readable holdings data as a permanent resource, one that requires maximum flexibility to be permanently and increasingly useful. The decision was made to use the emerging USMARC standard as the basis for development of a new Harvard holdings system.

HOLLIS

Mounting an online acquisitions system for such a diverse group of libraries was a massive project, and the implementation of MARC holdings was only a small part of it. After investigating several options ranging from complete in-house development to the purchase of a commercially marketed turnkey system, the Library decided to take a middle course. NOTIS, a powerful integrated system developed at Northwestern University, was chosen as the basis for extensive local modification. Fund accounting and invoice control were added, indexing and acquisitions functions enhanced, and an interface with the Union Catalog designed. The entire project, from technical specification to implementation, took two years to complete and an estimated 10-11 man-years of effort.

HOLLIS processing is based on three types of records: bibliographic, order, and holdings. Bibliographic records can be displayed online in their fully tagged and encoded form, and for the most part use standard MARC content designation. One important locally defined variation is the LOC field. This contains information specific to a particular copy of a title, such as holding library, call number, and local notes. When more than one Harvard unit holds a title, LOC fields for each holding unit are added to a single copy of the bibliographic record. (In NOTIS, a ''copy holdings'' record fulfills the same function.) LOC fields also contain linkages to a unit's order and holdings records for the item. One holdings record and up to 256 orders may be associated with a single LOC.

Order records are used for creating printed purchase orders and claims, recording receipt and payment, and for checking in currently received serials. A series of free-form text fields, called receipt lines, are used for serial check-in. When the volume is bound (or when the order record grows too long and unwieldy), check-in information is manually transferred to the holdings record and deleted from the order screen.

Holdings records are used to store holdings of nonunitary publications and also for local or copy-specific information about single-volume items, such as physical format and local notes. Information from the holdings record is reformatted and combined with data from the associated LOC field in generating a display for the Union Catalog. In HOLLIS, however, the holdings record can only be viewed in its fully tagged and encoded form. An example of the HOLLIS screen displays for a periodical and its associated order and holdings records is given in Figure 1.

It should be reiterated that the Harvard implementation of the USMARC holdings format constitutes a relatively simple and straightforward application. The holdings record is not used for recording current receipts or related check-in functions such as claiming or prediction of next expected issue. Data is not automatically transferred to the holdings record from receipt lines in the order record, and there is no automatic compression or expansion. Holdings data is entered and viewed online with full MARC content designation, and at present it is not reformatted for public display in real time.

There were several reasons for taking such a conservative approach to the holdings record and to serial control in general. More than half of the periodicals represented in the Union Catalog are not English language publications, and the percentage increases when nonunitary monographs are included. A relatively high proportion of the titles are irregularly published and/or received, or are obtained through exchange programs or other exceptional means. There was some concern on the part of the working groups designing HOLLIS serial functions that any automatic features relying on regular and predictable publication patterns would require frequent overriding, and might even be detrimental to some units with highly irregular collections. It was judged prudent to postpone the design of more sophisticated system features until there was more operational experience with online serial control.

66 THE USMARC FORMAT FOR HOLDINGS AND LOCATIONS

```
LTHU SAME                                              AAR6883
                                       LI812--HOLLIS CATALOGING  HP00
HU FMT: S ENCL: I C/DT: 04/27/82 U/DT: 06/13/86 STAT: n LGD: as DCF: a CHK: 5
LCALT:   LCCLAS:    0000 SRCH:   PUB ST: c PDT1: 19uu PDT2: 9999 CNTRY: ii
FREQ: f LANG: eng S/TYP: p REG: r ISDS:   MED:   REPROD:   CNTNT:      GOV:
CONF: 0 TP: u INDX: u CUMUX: u ALPHBT: a S/L: 0 MODREC:   CATSRC: d

035/1:0 : $a 08373712
040:   : $c HUL
245:00: $a Journal of advanced zoology.
260:01: $a Gorakhpur, India : $b Association for the Advancement of Zoology,
300:   : $a v. : $b ill. ; $c 27 cm.
310:   : $a Semiannual
500/1: : $a Description based on: Vol. 2, no. 2 (Dec. 1981); title from cover.
710/1:20: $a Association for the Advancement of Zoology (India)
LOC/1:9c: $i mcz $b JOU 3882
    MD: 04/27/82  H-1  BN-001-01


-------------------------------------------------------------------------
LTHU SAME                                              AAR6883-001
                                       LI812--HOLLIS CATALOGING  HP00
Journal of advanced zoology. -- Gorakhpur, India : Association for the
  Advancement of Zoology,
  LOC/1:9c: mcz $b JOU 3882
HU CREATED 01/19/85 UPDATED 06/13/86 FORMAT: H RECSTAT n RECTYP: y
LVL: 4 STAT: 4 METH: g RET: 8    COM: 1 COP: 01 CAN:     LANG:

852/1:  : $x Received via PL-480
853/2:13: $6 1 $a v. $b no. $u 02 $v r $i (year)
863/3:40: $6 1 $a 1-5 $i 1980-1984 $p B

-------------------------------------------------------------------------
LTHU DONE                                              AAR6883
                                       LI842-HOLLIS ACQUISITIONS HP00
 HU FMT: S ENCL: I CHK: 5 LANG: eng S/TYP: p FREQ: f
Journal of advanced zoology. -- Gorakhpur, India : Association for the
  Advancement of Zoology,
  LOC/1:9c: mcz $b JOU 3882
HO#: 001AAR6883  12/10/85 ORDUNIT: mz RECUNIT: 28 SCOPE: 2
VENDOR: X          ACTINT: 0400 POP: x L1:     L2:
VA:

NV:
NO: Received from PL-480 via Widener Serial Records
SOURCE:                          REF:
DIV 01 chk=v.:no. (year)
                                                      MED:    PCS:
001 BN                    E$:      0.00 E#: 00 MD 12/10/85 AD: NONE
    ACU:         CUR: usd AMT:             C#: 01 XPM: g L3/4:
003 R  v.6:no.1-2 (1985)                      MD 06/16/86 AD: 07/21/87
```

FIGURE 1. A HOLLIS bibliographic record and its associated holdings and order records.

THE CONVERSION PROJECT

While functional analysis and technical development for HOL-LIS was proceeding, a massive serials conversion project was also launched. The goals were to create a unified database of serials held at Harvard, to allow participating units to maintain their check-in and holdings records online, and to provide current bibliographic and holdings information to the Union Catalog. For units planning to use HOLLIS for serial check-in, the goal was to provide a bibliographic record for every currently received title, along with an open order record and enough retrospective holdings information to enable staff to perform 90% of their serial records activities online. An early study by a task group determined that in most cases the entire paper serial record would have to be converted, and that holdings would have to be reported at the detailed level for the paper record to be discarded.

A serials project coordinator was hired to oversee the conversion of both bibliographic and holdings data. The first decision to be made in planning for holdings conversion was whether to have a team of central project staff visit each unit to convert its paper records, or to have each library do its own conversion with existing operational staff. A "roving" project team would presumably develop significant expertise in encoding holdings data, but it would also have to learn the local files and practices at each library. Preliminary analysis determined that as much as the planning group liked the idea of roving bands of librarians, there was too much variation between the units for this to be practicable. It was also felt that the conversion process would be good training for operational staff ultimately responsible for the ongoing creation and maintenance of holdings data.

A pilot project was undertaken to ascertain the average cost of converting all paper holdings information for a title to the US-MARC format. Three units that differed widely in the characteristics of their serial collections and the form of their paper records were chosen as test sites. A training document was written, and one professional and three clerical staff members were trained in the use of the format. This team then visited each test site, transcribing samples of the unit's paper records onto workforms. The workforms were reviewed and corrected by the librarian, and entered into machine-readable form by the clerical staff.

Two methods of data entry were employed. Worksheets from one location were keyed using key-to-disk equipment that had previously been used to create MARC holdings for the old HUL Holdings File. Very little editing or data verification was done by the system, and when printouts of these records were proofread, over 70% of them were found to contain keying errors. Workforms from the other two test sites were entered online using a copy of NOTIS that had been installed when the decision was made to base HOLLIS on NOTIS software. These records were not formally reviewed, but the error rate was perceived to be significantly lower.

Separate counts were kept of titles completed per hour for each activity: transcription, revision, keying, and proofreading. In addition, it was determined that one out of every six records transcribed raised some problem that required review by a supervisor. The final figures used to derive a cost estimate were:

encoding	10 titles/hour
keying	15 titles/hour
review and correction	6 titles/hour
supervisory review	5 problems/hour, 1 problem per 6 titles

Unfortunately, when this was translated into cost per title converted using the current library pay scale, the figure obtained turned out to be more than the project could afford if all participating libraries were to be fully converted. In the end, the serial records of the largest potential participant, representing about 30,000 periodicals, were eliminated from the project. Staff within the other units were then trained by the project coordinator, and libraries were reimbursed from project funds on a per title basis.

For the initial holdings database, 61,000 records from the old HUL Holdings File were converted by program to the USMARC format. Whenever possible, 853 and 863 fields were constructed. The displaying form that would have been generated from the old holdings record was built and inserted as an 866 field of the new record. The second indicator of the 863 field was set to cause this 866 to be used for display in the Union Catalog whenever the program could determine that data had been lost in the conversion. Otherwise, the indicator was set to allow the display to be generated

Priscilla L. Caplan 69

from the 853/863 field pairs. The information that the record was machine-converted from the old HUL Holdings File was put into a nonpublic note subfield of the 852. Figure 2 shows examples of some HOLLIS holdings records converted by program from the old HUL Holdings File.

Since the pilot project pointed up the advantages of online data entry, and HOLLIS was still under development and not yet usable as a system, the NOTIS software was modified to allow holdings data entry. NOTIS performs table-based verification of field tags and subfields, so a special holdings table was constructed, and an additional editing routine was written to perform more extensive editing and cross-checking between fields. The machine-converted holdings were loaded into this system in July 1984, and participat-

```
LTHU SAME                                          AAP6593-001
                                    LI812--HOLLIS CATALOGING  HP00
Boletim de zoologia e biologia marinha. -- v. 26-30 (no. 1-4); 1970-73. --
   Numbers for [1971-73] issued by the Departamento de Fisiologia Geral with the
   Departamento de Zoologia and the Instituto de Biologia Marinha, Universidade
   de Sao Paulo.
   LOC/1:9c: mcz $b BOL 1432
HU CREATED 01/19/85 UPDATED 01/19/85 FORMAT: H RECSTAT n RECTYP: y
LVL: 4 STAT: 0 METH: u RET: 0     COM: 0 COP: 01 CAN:        LANG:

   852/1:   : $x m-c HHF E
   853/2:03: $6 1 $a v. $g no. $i (year)
   863/3:40: $6 1 $a 26-30 $g 1-4 $i 1970-1973
   866/4:40: $6 1 $a v.26-v.30 (no.1-no.4) ; 1970-1973

-------------------------------------------------------------------------

   LTHU SAME                                         AA01885-001
                                    LI812--HOLLIS CATALOGING  HP00
Zoologica africana. -- v. 1-   Mar. 1965- -- Published for the Zoological
   Society of Southern Africa with the aid of grants from the Dept. of Education,
   Arts and Science.
   LOC/1:9c: mcz $b ZOO 8584
HU CREATED 01/19/85 UPDATED 01/19/85 FORMAT: H RECSTAT n RECTYP: y
LVL: m STAT: 0 METH: u RET: 0     COM: 0 COP: 01 CAN:        LANG:

   852/1:   : $x m-c HHF E $z v.1 no.1 is xerox copy.
   853/2:03: $6 1 $a v. $b no. $i (year)
   863/3:32: $6 1 $a 1-13 $i 1965-1978
   866/4:40: $6 1 $a v.1-v.12:2, v.13:2 ; 1965-1978
```

FIGURE 2. Two HOLLIS holdings machine-converted from the old HUL Holdings File. The second will use the alternate form of display in the 866 field for Union Catalog display, as the second level of enumeration was lost in conversion.

70 THE USMARC FORMAT FOR HOLDINGS AND LOCATIONS

ing units with large numbers of active serials to convert used it to correct and enhance their machine-converted records and to create new records where none existed.

In July 1985, when the HOLLIS production system came online, this NOTIS holdings database underwent yet another format conversion and became the initial HOLLIS holdings database. Those libraries which had "preconverted" their holdings updated their records for very current receipts, while the remaining project participants added their holdings information directly into the HOLLIS database. By the end of the project in January 1986, approximately 90,000 MARC holdings records had been added to the database.

It is difficult to judge how closely the estimated cost per title approximated the actual expenses of the conversion participants. For obvious reasons, units with a high proportion of foreign language titles or relatively complicated, lengthy, or incomplete holdings spent more than those units with simpler records. In general, the perception is that on average the reimbursement did cover most of the labor expenses involved, although the costs of materials and some supervisory staff time were absorbed by the participating libraries.

TRAINING, DOCUMENTATION, AND STANDARDS

At the time of the conversion project, the only documentation available for the holdings format was a draft version of the USMARC standard. This could not be used without modification because of some local additions and variations in our implementation. Also, the project felt it was important for staff to understand the relationship between the MARC record in its encoded form and the way these holdings would display in the Union Catalog. The entire draft standard was rekeyed to reflect Harvard's version of the record, and examples were inserted after every field to show both the HOLLIS screen display and the resulting catalog display.

The revised holdings manual became part of the permanent documentation for the HOLLIS production system, and was recently reviewed and extensively revised. The most common complaint from the units was that the manual, organized in numerical order of field tags, was inadequate for both training and reference usage for a format in which MARC fields are so closely interdependent. The new version groups related fields so that, for example, the 853, 863, and 866 are documented consecutively. An introduction was added giving an overview of the holdings record structure and the relationship between fields, and many more examples and explanatory notes were inserted in the text. Four appendices now give Harvard standards for reporting, approved abbreviations for captions and chronology, a detailed explanation of how the Union Catalog display is derived, and 28 more pages of examples (Figure 3). With the holdings format, one example is worth a thousand words.

During the conversion project, each participating unit received three sessions of holdings training. The first session gave a general introduction to the format with particular attention to the fixed fields, the 853 and the 863. The second session converted sample records from that unit's paper files onto worksheets, and the third provided a hands-on demonstration of the online system by actually entering the data from the worksheets. At least two formal follow-up sessions were scheduled at each unit for questions and answers, and for the first 3 months of the project all new input was reviewed by the project coordinator. Records with encoding errors were printed and returned to the unit with an explanation of the problem. After the 3-month period, random samples were drawn regularly to continuously monitor quality.

Currently, holdings training is done as part of overall HOLLIS instruction for library staff. Each participating unit must designate two individuals as HOLLIS "liaisons," contact people for information and education about the system. Liaisons are fully trained by central University Library staff, and they are then responsible for training other HOLLIS operators at their own units. Five formal training sessions, including one 3-hour holdings workshop, cover all aspects of searching, data entry, acquisitions, and serials control.

PROBLEMS AND ISSUES

Before the new holdings format could be implemented, the draft USMARC standard was reviewed and in some instances modified to suit local needs. Throughout this period the Harvard systems

72   THE USMARC FORMAT FOR HOLDINGS AND LOCATIONS

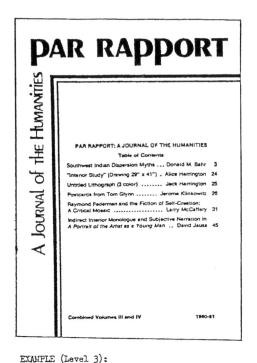

EXAMPLE (Level 3):

HOLLIS data:

   853:00: $6 1 $a v. $i (year/year)
   863:30: $6 1 $a 3/4- $i 1980/1981-

DUC display:

   Library has: v.3/4- - (1980/1981-   ), and current receipts.

EXAMPLE (Level 4):

HOLLIS data:

   853:00: $6 1 $a v. $i (year/year)
   863:41: $6 1 $a 3/4 $i 1980/1981 $w n
   863:40: $6 1 $a 7/8-9/10 $i 1984/1985-1986/1987

DUC display:

   Library has: v.3/4 (1980/1981); v.7/8-9/10 (1984/1985-1986/1987), and current receipts.

FIGURE 3. A page from the *Hollis Holdings Editing Guide*.

office was in close contact with MARBI and other groups involved with implementing and refining the holdings format, most notably the SEARL Holdings Committee. Several of Harvard's local variations were eventually accommodated in later drafts of the standard. These include the definition of a subfield $x ("Note (Nonpublic)") in fields 852 and 863-868, and the addition of subfield $g ("Gap/ nongap break indicator") in fields 863-865.

In initially adopting the new holdings format, the University Library was brave but not fearless. The road to Hell is paved with good intentions, and Harvard University Library's intentions were good enough to cause concern over which direction it was headed. Many librarians were afraid that the format was simply too complicated to be maintained by nonprofessional staff, while at the same time they feared it was not complex enough to handle any but the simplest publication patterns. After institutionally surviving the conversion project and a year of operational experience with the format, it seems that such fears were largely unfounded. More than 20 Library units are now successfully building and maintaining their own MARC holdings data online, and the database has grown to more than 105,000 records.

This does not, however, imply that the road to standardization is without its share of pitfalls and booby traps. For one thing, the format does require a certain amount of hand-holding, troubleshooting, and policy-making. Central staff in the University Library now includes one full-time serial holdings specialist. For ongoing quality control, a sample of all new and modified holdings records is reviewed weekly, and errors are reported to the responsible units for correction. The perception is that the error rate, which was constant for nearly a year after implementation, is now decreasing, and that the most common errors now have more to do with the derivation of Union Catalog display than with the proper encoding of enumeration and chronology.

A subcommittee of the Harvard Standing Committee on Bibliographic Standards and Policy is charged with setting standards and guidelines for holdings reporting. Perhaps the greatest ongoing problem is the lack of a nationally accepted set of rules for holdings similar to AACR2 for bibliographic data. Neither the draft US-MARC Format nor the *American National Standard for Serial*

74 THE USMARC FORMAT FOR HOLDINGS AND LOCATIONS

Holdings Statements (ANS Z39.44-1986) is comprehensive enough to offer guidance in any but the most common cases. There are also instances where the standards are clear but the resulting report is widely considered to be inadequate or confusing. When such a problem or question is shared by a number of Library units, the standards committee is asked to issue guidelines for that particular case. This ensures consistency in reporting within the University Library, but it causes concern about the exchangeability of data with other institutions.

For example, it is not uncommon for periodicals to have continuous numbering as the second level of enumeration. When the primary and secondary levels are recorded in the 863 subfields $a and $b and no gaps exist, the rules for compression cause the subfield $b to be omitted when the volume is complete. The continuous numbering would then be lost, despite the fact that citations to the title might refer to the continuous numbering only.

Another example concerns the recording of chronology when a volume spans more than a 12-month period. When no gaps exist, the required "year/year" notation in 863 subfield $i is sufficient to identify a library's holdings. When there are gaps, however, the notation can be ambiguous even when the date on the piece is straightforward; "February 1983," for example, might be displayed as:

1983/1984:Feb.

Internal guidelines have been issued to ameliorate both of these problems and several others, but it is unlikely that another institution using MARC holdings would independently arrive at identical solutions. The Library also has had to invent ways to record holdings of multivolume monographs, which are not yet addressed by the holdings format at all. Continuations, works-in-parts, loose-leaf publications, and items with replacement parts give rise to continual problems that will hopefully be resolved when the *American National Standard for Holdings Statements for Non-Serial Items*, now a draft standard of ANSI Z39 Subcommittee W, is integrated into the USMARC format.

Another problem concerns the double use of holdings records as both catalog and processing data. While bibliographic records are subject to stringent rules for accuracy and notation, and order records are locally defined to serve technical services needs, holdings records fall somewhere in between, and this schizophrenia is reflected by ongoing arguments over standards. Catalogers feel the holdings record should be consistent with cataloging data, so, for example, enumeration parallels the bibliographic 362, and new 853 fields are built for new captions. Serial records staff, on the other hand, can hardly keep up with meaningful changes in publication patterns. Harvard policy has been to take a middle ground, but practice varies widely from unit to unit.

The physical length of records is another ongoing concern. When the decision was made to use the MARC holdings format to replace paper serial records, units were committed to reporting very long runs, often with many gaps in holdings, at the detailed level. The design of the format proliferates 863 fields whenever a gap occurs, resulting in many extremely long holdings records. HOLLIS holdings records are subject to system-enforced maximums of 8185 characters to a record, 2048 characters to a field, and 255 fields with a single tag or within certain specified tag ranges. Many holdings records would exceed these limitations, and units must occasionally create two or more holdings records to represent a single serial run. For public display units are encouraged to enter summary statements in the 866 field, but this makes the record even longer and obligates staff to enter and maintain both the summary and the detailed notation. So far the Advisory Group has upheld the requirement for positive reporting in accordance with the MARC draft and ANS Z39.44-1986, but the single most common complaint of library staff is the absence of a provision for negative reporting.

The definition of compressibility and expandability is a problem the Library has ameliorated to some extent by announcing no intent to compress or expand holdings statements in the foreseeable future. Most Library units enter holdings in compressed form to begin with, and it is uncertain whether automatic expansion is either feasible or desirable. However, in order to be able to share holdings data with other institutions, units are encouraged to encode the first indicator of the 853 and 854 fields accurately according to the guidelines in the draft USMARC format. The problem is both conceptual and technical. "Compressibility" actually depends on the al-

76 THE USMARC FORMAT FOR HOLDINGS AND LOCATIONS

gorithm being used for compression, and it is not only conceivable but likely that different institutions will have different algorithms for performing the same function. To that extent, compressibility is local processing information, and has meaning only within a given system. A second way of looking at compressibility, and the approach taken by the draft USMARC format, is to define a certain amount of information as globally necessary for compression, and to set the indicator based on whether that information is supplied. While this does not mean the holdings are compressible in any particular system, it is actually the only practical way for operational staff to supply the indicator value. The problem here is that there are known cases in which the guidelines for compressibility are satisfied, but the holdings themselves are unlikely to be compressible. These difficulties are exaggerated in the case of expandability, about which even less is known.

A final major concern is the incompatibility between the display format prescribed by the *American National Standard for Serial Holdings Statements* and the structure of the content designation in the MARC holdings record. The ANSI standard specifies that chronology for each specific piece must directly follow enumeration for the piece in a compressed or uncompressed detailed statement, e.g.,:

v.1 (1976)-v.3 (1978)

This would be represented in USMARC as:

853    $a v. $i (year)
863    $a 1-3 $i 1976-1978

Although it is algorithmically possible to analyze the MARC 863 and reformat it according to ANS specifications, there is a serious concern about the amount of computing resources required, particularly if this were to be done in real time for an online public access catalog. Harvard therefore designed a much more straightforward display for its Union Catalog:

v.1-3 (1976-1978)

Although the decision to deviate from the standard was made with great reluctance, response from both librarians and patrons has been so favorable that one can question whether the prescribed ANS display is worth the amount of work required to obtain it.

The University Library is hopeful that most of the issues involving rules for encoding and display will ultimately be resolved as standards work progresses. Despite these problems, the HOLLIS implementation of the USMARC format can be considered a success. The Library now has a permanent database of high-quality holdings information, the ability to maintain and manipulate it, and the powerful promise of exchanging holdings information with other institutions.

NOTE

1. "Harvard Plans for Cooperation with Itself," *LJ/SLJ hotline* 9, no. 10 (10 March 1980):3.

Implementation and Use of the *USMARC Format for Holdings and Locations* at the University of Georgia Libraries

Greg Anderson

Through initial implementation and continued development of the *USMARC Format for Holdings and Locations*, the University of Georgia Libraries have derived substantial benefits which create the opportunity for automated control of its large collection of serials. This paper will address four areas regarding the use of the format at the University of Georgia Libraries. First, the environment for library automation at the University of Georgia will be described. Next, the decisions to implement the format will be discussed, followed by our initial steps toward use of the format. Finally, the current use and development projects for further utilization of the format at Georgia will be detailed.

LIBRARY AUTOMATION AT THE UNIVERSITY OF GEORGIA

The University of Georgia is the nation's first state-chartered institution of higher education. As the capstone institution for the University System of Georgia, the University has an enrollment of 25,000 students in 13 schools and colleges. The University of Georgia Libraries ranks in the top 30 ARL libraries; its collections ex-

---

Greg Anderson is Systems Librarian, University of Georgia Libraries.

80   THE USMARC FORMAT FOR HOLDINGS AND LOCATIONS

ceed 2.4 million, with 49,000 titles on subscription or standing order; and it has a materials budget of $3.4 million.

MARVEL (Management of Resources for University Libraries) is an integrated library automation system developed jointly by the University of Georgia Libraries and the Office of Computing and Information Services (OCIS), University of Georgia. Implemented in 1978, MARVEL is essentially a library automation application supported by a large database management system. MARVEL is fully integrated, and currently supports functional areas for collection development, ordering and receiving, fund accounting, circulation, and an online catalog. Cataloging is not yet supported through the MARVEL system; however, a development project to load and maintain our OCLC archival records in the MARVEL system is nearing implementation.

Before discussing the use of the holdings format in MARVEL, the structure of records in the MARVEL system requires some explanation. The system uses a relational database; elements of a record reside in various files (ca. 60) and are retrieved, formatted, and displayed for each query based upon the profile of the user. The hierarchy of records in MARVEL consists of three levels: SET, representing multi-unit records such as serials and series; TITLE, corresponding generally to the monographic level of bibliographic description; and PIECE, representing the physical entity which circulates through the system. Set and Title records also have location records which represent fund accounting data. Records are related appropriately to each other through a linkage structure implemented by the database management system (Figure 1). MARVEL currently contains over 500,000 bibliographic records; utilization of the OCLC archival records, including retrospective conversion records, will increase the size of the MARVEL database dramatically.

Support for library automation activities at Georgia has been very strong. The Libraries have enjoyed close communication and extensive support from OCIS. Currently six programmers on the staff of OCIS comprise the Library Automation group providing applications programming and systems support to MARVEL. The MARVEL system operates on an IBM 3081-D (shared) mainframe. Communications control for MARVEL is handled by CICS (Cus-

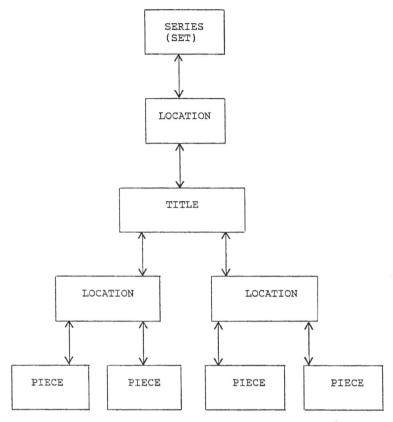

FIGURE 1. MARVEL record structure and relationship.

tomer Information Control System), and all database files are managed by an Integrated Catalog Facility.

DECISION TO IMPLEMENT THE USMARC FORMAT FOR HOLDINGS AND LOCATIONS

Our decision to implement the format was based externally on a U.S. Office of Education Title II-C grant received in 1981 and internally on an approach to solve a MARVEL system architecture problem. The Title II-C grant was made to eight Southeastern ARL libraries who proposed three objectives:

1. Initial development of a regional resource sharing system for serials;
2. Creation of machine notation for a detailed serial holdings statement; and,
3. Improvement of cooperative collection development and resource sharing among the involved libraries.

Of course the interest in and implications of this machine notation for detailed holdings soon became apparent. The Library of Congress responded by agreeing to work with the participants in its development. This expanded scope and work culminated in the *USMARC Format for Holdings and Locations* published by the Library of Congress in 1984.

Implementation of the format presented options for capturing and displaying serial holdings in MARVEL. Without the format our relational database structure would have required additional levels of complexity and linkage. Such a structure would have been unwieldy for processing as well as for creating acceptable displays in the online catalog (Figure 2).

The format, however, presents an efficient mechanism for capturing and communicating holdings and locations data in a more linear fashion. The publication pattern information provides the necessary hierarchical information needed for manipulation and display (Figure 3).

This ability to address an area of concern by use of a standard was a key factor in our implementation decision. By focusing resources around the format, we can now pursue the goal of a functionally integrated, automated serials control module. The format provides opportunities for two basic objectives: continued development toward a totally online environment for library operations, and the capability to carry in a standard manner our machine-readable data forward into the future. At the time of our decision to implement the format, we chose not to address questions about the display of holdings data. Our initial intent was to utilize this MARC format for what it does best: mark, store, and communicate. With the flexibility provided by the format, we felt confident we could build a good display.

Implementation of the format also brought the realization that we

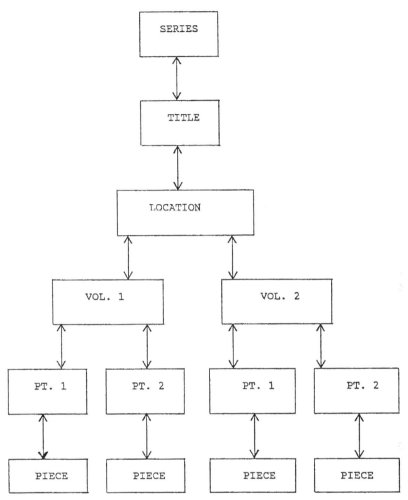

FIGURE 2. MARVEL structure for holdings *without* the format.

were "wedded" to it; that is, not only were we committed to creating holdings records based on the format, we were also committed to maintaining those records. This constant task appeared daunting at first. Those trepidations, however, have proved largely unfounded and are more a product of perspective than of actual experience. Maintenance of holdings records has involved updating detailed holdings, corresponding to level four of the *American*

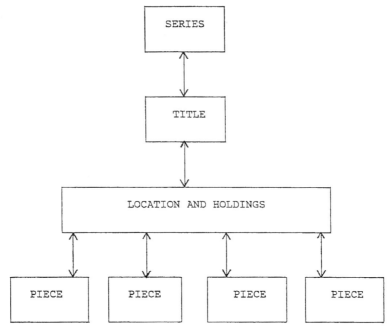

FIGURE 3. MARVEL holdings structure with the format.

National Standard for Serial Holdings Statements, ANSI Z39.44, as well as maintenance of each title's publication pattern (field 853). Maintenance of current and accurate field 853 information is fundamental to the communication, manipulation, and display of holdings.

IMPLEMENTATION AND CURRENT USE OF THE FORMAT

Detailed planning and initial programming for use of the format in the MARVEL system began in Fall 1984. The decision was made to first create and maintain holdings records for our current periodicals, because those materials do not circulate. Design and planning decisions were the responsibility of the Serials Group, an *ad hoc* committee composed of library and computer center staff. Working first from a draft and finally from the published format, this group was charged with interpreting the format and providing guidelines for its implementation. It has been our experience that the format as published does not provide clear guidelines; it does, however, provide numerous examples. These examples do not cover a very broad range of possibilities, and it is left to the reader to infer rules for the format based upon analysis of these somewhat simplified examples. Additional explanations and specific guidelines are needed.

Implementing the format in MARVEL requires a close distinction between those components of the format which are bibliographic and those which are local or location specific. In this instance the MARVEL record structure proved quite accommodating. Field 853 is regarded as bibliographic, remaining constant for that title regardless of location or holdings. For this reason, it was linked to the MARVEL SET record. Actual holdings information, fields 863-868, reflects data for a particular location, and the record representing this information is linked through the appropriate MARVEL location to the SET record (Figure 4).

Data gathering for creation of publication pattern and holdings information was accomplished by extracting data from automated and manual sources. MARVEL provided bibliographic data for each title and some pattern information. Publication patterns were more clearly defined through analysis of the manual kardex file records. Remaining aware of our internal goal for automated control of our serials, we decided to input data at the detailed level (level four) which records specific holdings at a location and incorporates all levels of enumeration and chronology. The serial card catalog provided most of the information needed to reflect this level, although some trips to the stacks were inevitable.

Acknowledging the fact that we would at times fill in gaps retrospectively (perhaps even with an earlier publication pattern), we began our sequence control numbering, subfield 6, for pairing fields 853/863 with the number eight. This has provided the flexibility to insert holdings from an earlier period by using a lower sequence control number. Because periodicals do not circulate, we have entered our retrospective holdings in a compressed form (Figure 5). Holdings records are updated as bound volumes return from the bindery.

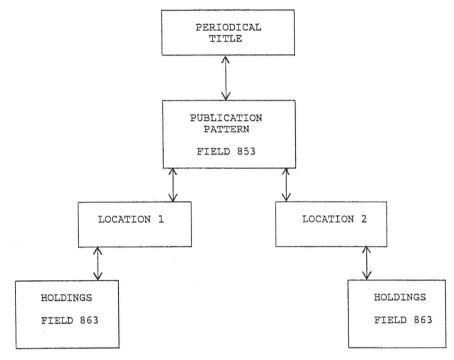

FIGURE 4. Holdings format as represented in MARVEL.

Field 866, designed primarily for the free text expression of holdings, has been used only when there is no discernible pattern information, or when the holdings are so complex and incomplete that no logical relationship between pattern and holdings can be determined. The format describes four possible uses for field 866; it has been used at Georgia where no 853/863 fields are present in the record and where fields 853/863 are used to record some of the holdings and field 866 is used for the remainder. This second use becomes necessary when, for a certain time period, there is no identifiable publication pattern or when the holdings are scattered or very complicated. This combined use of 853/863 and 866 data requires coordination of the sequence control number in subfield $6 for placement in the correct chronological sequence. More than 14,000 holdings records have been created and maintained at Georgia. Of those, however, only 800 contain field 866. Whenever pos-

Greg Anderson 87

```
853 12$68$aser.3:v.$bno.$u12

    $vr$i(year)$j(month)$wm

853 12$69$aser.3:v.$bno.$u6

    $vr-i(year)$j(month)$wm


863 40$68.10$a1-24$i1918-1941

863 40$68.11$a25$b2-10$i1942

863 40$68.12$a26$i1943

863 40$68.13$a27$b1-8$i1944

863 40$68.14$a27$b11-12$i1944

863 40$69.10$a28-99$i1945-1985

863 40$69.11$a100$b1-3$1985
```

FIGURE 5. Periodical holdings for a typical title.

sible, fields 853/863 were discerned for a record in order to maintain the flexibility and manipulation of the data which those fields provide. This ability to manipulate the holdings data is lost in the free text data entry of field 866 (Figure 6).

Creation and input of holdings records began in Winter 1985, with data having been input primarily by clerical staff. It has been our experience that once data gathering and publication pattern information are complete, actual data entry proceeds rapidly.

The data entry screen for field 863 provides some bibliographic information carried forward by the system and the latest field 853, containing pattern, caption, and sequence control information for that title. Entry of holdings data is accomplished by updating only those subfields of the last field 863. MARVEL will then produce a new field 863 based on the updated information. The "template" process greatly expedites this work (Figure 7).

Maintenance has embodied updating holdings at level four as well as work with each title's publication pattern. Our approach to communication and manipulation of holdings is keyed to pattern information. Location and call number information, found in field

```
                    866 HOLDINGS DATA
 EXAMPLE:O866TAG001>40¬60¬av.10 no.2-5(1973), v.12 no.1(1975)
 SET#>0000-782-261       SET>Armchair Bulletin       OWNLIB>GACG
 O866TAG001>40¬69¬a(1962:SPRING), (1963:FEB-MAR), (1963:NOV), (1964:MAR), (1964:
 MAY), (1964:FALL), (1965:FALL-WINTER), (1966:SPRING), (1966:FALL), (1967)

 O866TAG002>40¬69¬a(1968:FALL-WINTER), (1969:SPRING), v.2-3(1969/70-1970/71), v.
 4 no.1-2(1971/72), v.5 no.2(1972/73), v.6-8(1973/74-1975/76)


 OPTIONS: U-update; R-redisplay; CD-Cre. dsply;

 RESPONSE->
```

FIGURE 6. MARVEL data entry screen for field 866 (Note the sequence control number in subfield $6 for appropriate sequencing with fields 853/863 in this record).

```
                          863 HOLDINGS DATA
  EXAMPLE:O863TAG001>40┐61.1┐a10┐b1-12┐i1984┐j01-12
  853 STRING:12┐69┐aser.3:v.┐bno.┐u6┐vr┐i(year)┐j(month)┐wm
  SET#>0000-773-958        SET>American Journal of Ophthalmology       OWNLIB>GAZLM
       CALL#>RE1.A5              MLTIPART>Y      ENCLVL>4     RCACQST>4     MTHACQ>p
  CANCEL>____      GENRET>8      SPERET>____     COMPL>0    COPY>001    LEND>a      REPRO
>a     COMPOSIT>0
  O863TAG001>40┐68.10┐a1-24┐i1918-1941
  O863TAG002>40┐68.11┐a25┐b2-10┐i1942
  O863TAG003>40┐68.12┐a26┐i1943
  O863TAG004>40┐68.13┐a27┐b1-8┐i1944
  O863TAG005>40┐68.14┐a27┐b11-12┐i1944
  O863TAG006>40┐69.10┐a28-100┐i1945-1985
  O863TAG007>40┐69.11┐a101┐b1-6┐i1986


  OPTIONS: U-update; R-redisplay; CD-Cre. dsply;

  RESPONSE->
```

FIGURE 7. MARVEL data entry screen for field 863.

852 in the format, are already handled by data elements present in the MARVEL system. For the output of these records, however, those separate elements would be represented in field 852.

In the summer of 1985, attention was focused on the display of holdings information to staff and patrons. The pairing of field 853 and 863 provides the flexibility to crate virtually any display. This interaction between national level and local data is an exciting feature of the format. While the MARC format has always accommodated local and national level data in one record, those areas existed independently of each other. The holdings format, however, represents the first time in the MARC format that these types of data actually interact. The role of field 853 as bibliographic data is to determine the capture and communication of field 863, locally designated data. This relationship can also be expressed as one between designating terms and the actual values of those terms (Figure 8).

Public displays of holdings in the online catalog were determined by an analysis and review process involving staff from several areas. The display format chosen does not conform to *The American National Standard for Serial Holdings Statements* (ANSI Z39.44). To see holdings displays in the online catalog, a patron retrieves the desired title; holdings locations for that title are displayed with the bibliographic information. A location is chosen by a line number

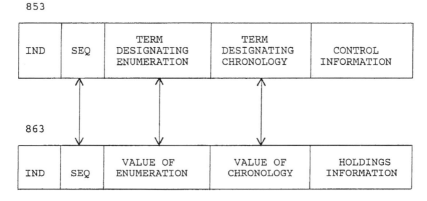

FIGURE 8. Relationship of fields 853/863 for display.

option, and the bound volume holdings for that location are displayed with location and shelving information (Figures 9 and 10). Public displays have been available since March, 1986; patron response has been favorable, and access provided to staff throughout the libraries has been very beneficial.

PRESENT DEVELOPMENT AND FUTURE USE OF THE FORMAT

In the past 2 years, we have become comfortable with the format and are pleased with how it handles our periodical titles. Within the scheme of our present automation priorities, the holdings format has a central role. One project currently underway is a test of the communication capability of the format.

To pursue further our objective for automated serials control, we are currently a beta test site for MicroLINX, a microcomputer based serials check-in system developed by The Faxon Company. The development of MicroLINX has been centered around the *US-MARC Format for Holdings and Locations*. By endorsing and supporting this standard, Faxon is providing a product which can interface with other systems which also support the format. As an economic and resource efficient model, this modular approach presents advantages over in-house development for a check-in function in MARVEL.

The University of Georgia Libraries has been a beta test site for MicroLINX since February, 1986. Initial testing has focused on the MicroLINX application in a large academic library setting. In addition, we are now beginning to test interfacing MicroLINX and MARVEL, using the holdings format as the communication agent. The goal of this work is to use MicroLINX for issue check-in; to upload this issue level information in the holdings format into MARVEL; and, finally, to add this data to the holdings record already maintained in the MARVEL system. Through this interface, we will provide online catalog patrons with issue level information for our periodicals (Figure 11).

At this writing, the most recent version of MicroLINX, version three, has been received and implemented. This version provides interface screens: records can be flagged for interfacing, and the

```
YOUR SEARCH: TITLE>AMERICAN JOURNAL OF OPHTHALMOLOGY          MATCHES:     1

TITLE:  American Journal of Ophthalmology

SUBJECTS:
Ophthalmology -- periodicals

***THIS IS A PERIODICAL. IF MULTIPLE LOCATIONS APPEAR BELOW, DETERMINE THE
   LOCATION OF INTEREST TO YOU. TO DISPLAY VOLUMES OWNED AT THAT LOCATION,
   TYPE IN ITS LINE NUMBER.

   1.  LOCATION: SCIENCE (4th)
       CALL#: RE1.A5
       NOTE: Current issue at Vet. Med. Reading Room for 30 days
       Current periodicals are in the Current Periodicals Room Science
```

```
OPTIONS: LINE#-display volume information;

RESPONSE-> 1                                              PAGE:    1
```

FIGURE 9. Online catalog screen showing Title and Location.

```
YOUR SEARCH: TITLE>AMERICAN JOURNAL OF OPHTHALMOLOGY          MATCHES:      1

  TITLE:   American Journal of Ophthalmology
  CALL#:   RE1.A5

  VOLUME LOCATION: SCIENCE (4th)
  VOLUMES: ser.3:v.1-24(1918-1941), ser.3:v.25 no.2-10(1942),
   ser.3:v.26(1943), ser.3:v.27 no.1-8(1944),
   ser.3:v.27 no.11-12(1944), ser.3:v.28-100(1945-1985),
   ser.3:v.101 no.1-6(1986)
  INDEXES: ser.3:v.26-35(1943-1952), ser.3:v.36-54(1953-1962),
   ser.3:v.55-74(1963-1972)
  SUPPLEMENTS: ser.3:v.1 pt.2(1918), ser.3:v.2 pt.2(1919), ser.3:v.11(1928)



  _____
  OPTIONS:   R-return to list of locations;

  RESPONSE->                                            PAGE:    1
```

FIGURE 10. Online catalog screen showing Holdings at a Location (Note: Display of index holdings created from 855/865 pairing; supplement holdings created from free text field 867).

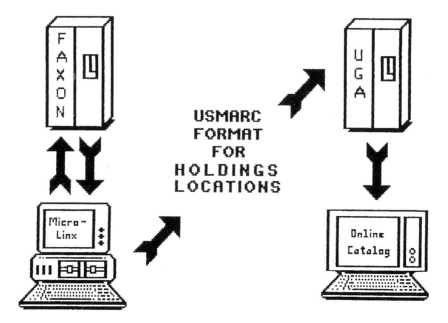

FIGURE 11. Representation of the interface test between MicroLINX and MARVEL.

MicroLINX user can then determine which interface to choose, e.g., a host system such as MARVEL, a union list, utility, etc. When the interface program is run, a record is output for each flagged title, containing numeric links to the record on the other end, the latest field 853, and the issue level information formatted into field 863.

Two basic requirements must be presented for this interface to succeed. First, the holdings record formatted in MicroLINX must be able to map properly to the corresponding record in MARVEL; second, the field 853 pattern information must match in both records to provide proper sequencing of the field 863 information.

Another requirement will be compression of data. If the issue level holdings remain as separate field 863s in the MARVEL holdings record, the holdings and display will become cumbersome. The format provides the ability to compress detailed level holdings into summary level holdings. At the time of interfacing, the MARVEL record will be required to check and accept the new field 863, and a new display for those holdings will be generated automatically.

A corresponding test involving MicroLINX and the holdings format is our test of the Serials Industry Systems Advisory Committee (SISAC) code. At present, MicroLINX will read this bar code and retrieve the corresponding record. Eventually, it will use the SISAC code to check-in the issue. The SISAC code is composed of the ISSN, chronology, and enumeration for the issue, with the capability to accommodate code for the page number and title code of individual articles. In addition to the code 128 bar code symbology, the SISAC code includes an eye-readable representation as well. Because MicroLINX is a predictive system, it will map the SISAC code into the appropriate segments of the holdings format, and, finding a match with the next issue expected for that title, the SISAC code will trigger check-in for the issue (Figure 12).

Our other current project concerning the format is its use with other serial and nonserial materials. Unlike periodicals, bound volumes of serials circulate through MARVEL. We must be able to integrate the holdings as represented in the format and the individual circulation activity for each volume. Subfield $p in field 863 will be used for the MARVEL bar code (accession) number, which is the key for our circulation record. Our goal is to represent holdings for a serial in a display and to display for patrons the circulation status for each piece. Another requirement for this development is the capability in MARVEL to receive these materials and add them to holdings records without duplication of effort (Figure 13).

Because of the MARVEL record structure described at the beginning of this paper, monographic sets and multivolume monographs are treated as MARVEL SETS. It is our intention to provide and support the holdings format at all appropriate levels of the MAR-

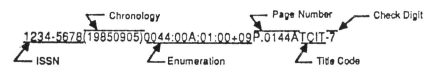

FIGURE 12. Components of SISAC code.

THE USMARC FORMAT FOR HOLDINGS AND LOCATIONS

```
853 10$61$avol.$bpt.$u2

863 51$61.1$a1$b1$p12345
863 51$61.2$a1$b2$p12346
863 51$61.3$a2$b1$p12347
863 51$61.4$a2$b2$p12348

Vol. 1 - 2
```

FIGURE 13. Representation of fields 853/863 including 863 $p for the accession number.

VEL structure. Monographic materials will then be handled in a more consistent manner.

RECOMMENDATIONS AND SUMMARY

Analysis of the format must continue. As more libraries begin use of the format, this increased body of knowledge will be very helpful. There appears to be some hesitation about implementing the format, which may be a reflection of concerns about the complexity of the format. On a national level, there are several opportunities for cooperation which may help ease the fears about the format and which may also benefit cooperative projects now in operation. Availability of pattern information (field 853) for loading into systems is crucial. Determination and national distribution of pattern information along with the remainder of the record's bibliographic data would provide opportunities for enriched communication of records. The communication of holdings information is tied to acceptance of the pattern for a title. The published format needs additional explanation and guidelines, and should address more complex examples. If there is the opportunity for true adherence to the format, these revisions are necessary soon.

The University of Georgia Libraries has had a positive experience implementing and using the format. As a component of our automation priorities, the format has facilitated progress in several areas. Our development projects presently in progress give us real prospects for achievement in the near future. By endorsing, implementing, and supporting the format we have been able to address several current areas of development as well as maintaining flexibility and options for future directions.

REFERENCES

USMARC Format for Holdings and Locations. Washington: Library of Congress, 1984.
"The Report of the Serials Industry Systems Advisory Committee." *SISAC News* 1, no. 1 (October 1985):27.

Adapting the *USMARC Format for Holdings and Locations* for Local Serials Control: The University of Kansas Serials System

John S. Miller

This is a case study of one university library's attempt to implement the new *USMARC Format for Holdings and Locations* as part of a locally developed, single-institution serials control system. It does not describe how to perform a pure implementation of the holdings format. Instead it shows the interaction of national standards with local needs, of almost unlimited demands with local constraints, of new content designation with old data, and of the desire for conformity to the format with the necessity of creating a working system in a given amount of time.

The local nature of the implementation is paramount for two reasons. First of all, the balance at the University of Kansas of existing local systems, data processing staff, money, and time set fairly firm limits on the new serials system's design. Second, local needs and functional priorities generally took precedence whenever a conflict seemed to exist between local needs and literal allegiance to the holdings format. We did not want to be limited by the format, especially since it was quite young and untested.

Creating a standard system that would allow the easy sharing of data was a high priority. This did not always mean, however, that the system would in all cases store and manipulate data using the exact form and content designation prescribed by the communica-

---

John S. Miller is Library Automation Analyst, University of Kansas Libraries.

tions format. The new system had to be first and foremost a local serials control system and had to accomplish the primary goals of the libraries' serials department. As the project and the programming developed, the most efficient and effective means to that end appeared to be to use the holdings format as a base, but not an inviolable base, and to add to it or change parts of it whenever necessary. We took seriously its status as a communications format. We believed we could make local variations and modifications and still communicate data in the national format by using record conversion programs. Our beginning assumptions and approach to this are discussed in more depth below.

This paper is divided into four parts: 1) a description of the local context at the University of Kansas; 2) an overview of the new serials system, including its general design and the decision to use the new holdings format; 3) a description of how the principles and the practice of the format are used in some of the central components of the serials system; and 4) some conclusions.

The third section is the longest and most important. It describes in detail the parts of the system that interact with the holdings record, stressing the functional goals of the system and how those goals affected the system design. It presents some of the specifics of Kansas' implementation of the holdings format, concentrating on problem areas, on additions and modifications that seemed to be necessary or useful, and on how the basic design and coding of the format influenced other parts of the system.

THE CONTEXT

At the time the new serials project began in earnest in early 1985, Kansas had in place: 1) a locally developed circulation system installed in 1979; 2) a locally developed cataloging, authority control, and COM catalog production system installed in 1984; 3) the IN-NOVACQ acquisitions system; and 4) a 15-year old, brief-record, mostly batch serials system running on a Honeywell computer that the University wished to discard by mid-1987. The new serials system was to be installed by late 1986 (which it was), with the next project to be an online catalog (a locally developed one is now projected for late 1987).

As is apparent from the list of systems, most library automation at Kansas is homegrown. There are at least three practical reasons for this: the working relationship between the library and the university computer center is very good and continues to improve; the library does not have to pay "real" money for computers, disk space, or for a number of other products and services; and there is a staff of three library programmers/analysts, all librarians, who work for the computer center, but dedicate their time to library projects. The local situation thus strongly favors developing customized local systems rather than buying more generalized systems from a vendor. The library has looked at commercial systems, but with the exception of an acquisitions system, has decided on local development.

Time and programming staff are both limited. The automation needs of a large academic library seem unlimited, both in the number and the scope of applications needed. Some institutions appear not to want a system until they can have the complete, "do-everything" system. That requires a great deal of time or money or both. Kansas has opted, mostly by necessity, for a more gradual, system-by-system, phased approach, with programming staff generally being assigned to one system at a time, with a firm deadline and with modest, practical goals. The negative side to this approach is that existing systems are enhanced too infrequently and the various modules are less well-integrated than in many other systems. The positive side is that we have good, practical, working systems in place, and we probably had them much sooner than would have been possible otherwise. In many cases, we also feel that their custom nature makes some of the systems more powerful and sophisticated than their equivalent modules in more integrated systems.

With the advent of the new serials system, all locally developed systems run on an IBM-compatible mainframe under the MVS operating system. Online programs use the CICS teleprocessing monitor. All files are simple VSAM files; there is no database management system. All batch programs were written in PL/l; the online serials system programs are in PL/l and assembler language; older online programs are in assembler and COBOL. The serials system consists of approximately 90 online programs and 25 batch programs.

THE NEW SERIALS SYSTEM

The driving force behind planning the serials system was two-fold: 1) for hardware replacement reasons the old serials system either had to be replaced or rewritten for a different computer; and 2) the old system was recognized as inadequate and obsolete. The obvious decision therefore was that we needed a new system, not a simple rewriting of the old system.

It was also clear that the bibliographic and holdings information in the records in the old system, despite its inadequacies, should somehow live on at least temporarily in the new system. It was not as clear, however, what the scope and functionality of the new system should be, nor how the new system would integrate with the existing cataloging/authority system.

At Kansas, decisions on a system's functions are usually made by a committee that includes librarians and programming staff. A committee began discussing the new serials system in mid-1984. The initial debate was quite heated. There was the customary creation of wish lists, the normal clash of priorities, and the usual arguments over quality versus quantity and national standards versus local practice that seem to be the inevitable course of most library automation projects. The principal obstacle was that at least the first phase of a new system had to be operational by the end of 1986. It would not be possible to build the perfect, all-inclusive system by that time. Eventually, the committee agreed to a compromise that recognized both the necessity of starting a project and the impossibility of doing everything right away. One of the programmers wrote a project plan and the discussion then turned to an elaboration of the basic plan.

One of the disputed points all along was to what extent the new nonbibliographic record and display formats would follow national standards. Holdings records in the old system had been in a thoroughly local format and the serials staff had presumed that the new format, although improved, would still be local. The full emergence of the new holding format at approximately the time the committee was considering the question forced the issue. Cataloging department personnel, who had been involved with shared cataloging and with the USMARC bibliographic and authorities formats for years, were the strongest advocates of adopting and using standard formats, including the holdings format. Some serials department staff were not convinced. They had four principal objections: 1) implementing the format would make programming much more difficult and would therefore limit the time available to work on other parts of the system; 2) the holdings record itself would be difficult to use and understand, both for public service staff and for serials technical service staff; 3) rigidly following the standard would not allow for certain types of local practice; and 4) the format, which records all holdings in a positive manner, would not accommodate the negatively expressed data from the old serials system.

To a greater or lesser extent, all four objections proved to be valid. But most of the objectionable points also proved to have positive aspects. Basing an automatic check-in system on the holdings format was rather difficult, but the format provided the structure for a fairly sophisticated prediction and update system. The holdings record is initially difficult to read and understand, but it is very versatile and its very cryptic nature forced us to include a very useful online translated version of the holdings record as part of the initial system.

The most serious objections were the last two: the format does not match certain types of local library practice and does not accommodate coded negative holdings. The committee decided that all newly recorded holdings should be positive holdings, but there was still the problem of data carried over from the old system that would only gradually be revised and recoded. We had to convert all the data, which was impossible, or develop a local format, or create a niche for negative holdings in the MARC holdings format.

This dilemma, combined with the strong urge to use the format if possible, led to the working compromise already alluded to. We would use the format, follow it as closely as possible, make additions and changes to cope with local processing patterns and local data and local programming realities, and where changes were made, try to allow for conversion of Kansas coding into standard coding. This pragmatic approach seemed logical and possible. Given more time and more creativity, we might have been able to

104 THE USMARC FORMAT FOR HOLDINGS AND LOCATIONS

serve our purpose with fewer modifications, but that is a moot point.

The current system that evolved from this process has the following components:

1. An online searching system providing browsable indexes, with access by all title, name, series, and linking entry fields, by all combinations of name + title or title + name, by ISSN, by record number, and by order number. The indexes are recreated nightly.
2. An online record editing system for creation and modification of both bibliographic and holdings records. Numerous types of local records can be created online. As titles are cataloged or recataloged on OCLC, their OCLC records enter the cataloging/authority and serials systems automatically from OCLC tapes (bumping any preliminary or old brief record in the process), and their headings are linked to the authority file.
3. An individual issue module that allows the user to create, edit, and retrospectively store several thousand issue records per copy (each record can be up to a full screen in size).
4. A check-in system that interacts directly with issue records and holdings records, automatically updating holding record fields, and when possible, creating new expected issues.
5. An online source or vendor file, with segments for multiple addresses, claiming control information, and billing and account records.
6. A claiming system that produces batch reports, shelf-check forms, and customized claim letters, and creates and maintains complete claiming histories in the individual issue records.
7. A monthly public COM central serials record with complete bibliographic information and complete holdings listed under all access points except subject headings.
8. A "reference holdings display" that is essentially a labeled display of brief bibliographic information plus the complete translation of the note and holdings fields in one copy's holdings record. This is both for public service staff and for serials staff who code holdings records and wish to check their work.

The screen is recreated each time it is displayed so any changes are immediately reflected online. This display will be the basis for the future public online catalog's serials holdings display. (An example appears in Figure 2 of Appendix B at the end of this paper.)

9. A custom report system that provides offline printing of records matching one or more of numerous criteria such as vendor, language, country of origin, call number range, location, last-update date, etc. The report selection and sorting criteria are requested on an online form.

The project also included the conversion programs that attempted to turn the old bibliographic and holdings data into MARC records.

What the new system lacks is an ordering and accounting module, a binding module, and an automatic interface with the circulation system. Order and binding information is stored in the holdings record and appears on reports, but for the moment it is for informational purposes only.

THE HOLDINGS FORMAT IN THE SYSTEM

This section describes the problems and functional requirements that shaped the Kansas adaptation and implementation of the holdings format. All additions and modifications occurred in response to specific problems. The description concentrates on three topics: 1) the conversion of old records into new MARC-like records; 2) the different types of records in the new system and their relationships; and 3) the check-in and issue update system that predicts new issues and updates holdings record fields. All three parts discuss coding modifications, additions, and requirements.

Conversion of Old Holdings

The library's old machine-readable serials records included brief bibliographic data, holdings data, and a variety of fund, claiming, binding, and purchase data all in one short, fixed-length, all uppercase record. Each copy had a separate record, so one title might have two or more records. One record, however, contained the complete run of a copy, both bound and unbound, even if the copy's run was spread across two or three locations. Some parts of the old record had unambiguous content designation, others did not. Almost all holdings were expressed as a combination of first and last issue held with a list of missing issues, for example, "1950-1975, lacking 1967, 1969-1971, 1974."

An early topic of heated debate was whether the new system would maintain the practice of expressing holdings negatively or would switch to positive holdings. The committee made the decision to move to positive holdings before it discussed the holdings format. This decision was crucial and made it possible to consider implementing the holdings format.

It was clear, however, that the old negatively expressed holdings could not be automatically turned into positive holdings due to the lack of complete publication pattern histories. At the same time, we were not about to discard the old data or manually rework all of it before beginning the new system. Therefore, the new system, regardless of what holdings format it used, would have to accommodate both old negative holdings and new positive holdings.

This decision forced the first two additions to the format. First of all, we needed a negative holdings field. We considered using the 866, but did not like its lack of content designation. Instead we created the 869 field, coded to match our old holdings, parallel in as many ways as possible to the regular 863 field.

Because the 869 field basically follows the 863 model, it needed a companion 853 field. We made coding changes to the 853 field to match the 869. In brief, subfield $a of such an 853 field contains a one-level or two-level enumeration, separated by a colon; subfield $i contains a one-level or two-level chronology, also separated by a colon; and subfield $m contains a string of lacking issues (matching the captions in subfield $a).

Indicating that a particular 853 field defined an 869 rather than a standard 863 holdings field prompted the second addition. The third indicator was born, eventually becoming part of all variable fields in the format. All variable fields thus have three indicators, whether they need them or not (many do need them). The first two indicators retain their normal meanings; the third contains local processing or informational data.

Example of 853/869 coding for a monthly with holdings of

"Vol. 5, no. 1 (Jan. 1975)-vol. 12, no. 6 (June 1982)

Lacking: vol. 7, no. 3; vol. 9, no. 2'':

```
853  . . .    $a vol.:no. $i (year:month) $w m
869  . . .    $a 5:1-12:6 $i 1975:01-1982:06 $m 7:3, 9:2
```

Record Types and Relationships

An early, basic decision was that the new system should have three separate principal types of records: bibliographic records, holdings records, and individual issue records. Their definitions and relationships had a number of effects on Kansas' implementation of the MARC holdings format.

First of all, *bibliographic records* were to be more or less generic records representing only the original format of a serial. There would be only one bibliographic record per title, not one per format or per copy. Holdings records thus would have to contain more information, such as physical format and publishing information, than if there were to be a separate bibliographic record for each format.

Second, new *holdings records* were to be one for each copy of a title, with the ability to hold the entire run of a copy in one record. Keeping an entire run in one record was seen as very important, especially for public access and binding update reasons. The typical situation is for the more recent years of a serial to be in the Periodicals Reading Room, with older years in the stacks. Separate subscriptions that make up one "copy," such as a hard copy subscription that is replaced by microfilm, have separate nonpublic holdings records for ordering, check-in, and claiming purposes, but the total holdings are also combined in one record for public display.

The library's desire to keep a run together directly contradicts the holding format's declaration that the 852 field is not repeatable if detailed holdings are coded. We either had to change our minds, devise some elaborate set of linked holdings records, or make the 852 field repeatable. The latter seemed the best solution. The 852 thus became fully repeatable, acquiring its own subfield $6 sequence code. Each 852 begins with a sequence letter ("a" to "z").

108 *THE USMARC FORMAT FOR HOLDINGS AND LOCATIONS*

The 85x and 86x fields related to a particular 852 field have the 852 sequence letter added to the front of their subfield $6 sequence number. Using a letter seemed preferable to adding another level of numbers to the sequence numbers in the 85x and 86x fields. The first 852 field is thus "a," its first 853 field is "al," the first 863 field is "al.1." The standard sequencing and Kansas's alternative appear as follows:

Normal 852/853/863 combination:

852   0 1 $a KKU $b KKUA . . .

853   2 0 $6 1 $a vol. $b no. . . .

863   4 0 $6 1.1 $a 1-3 $b 1-6

Kansas adaptation:

852   0 1 1 $6 a $a KKU $b KKUA . . .

853   2 0 1 $6 al $a vol. $b no. . . .

863   4 0 1 $6 al.1 $a 1-3 $b 1-6

The third indicator was useful in this new multi-852 situation in that it allowed us to code the physical format of the 852-group holdings.

The 852 field became repeatable only after it seemed reasonably certain that a multi-852 field holdings record could be communicated as several single-852 field records without losing anything significant. Again, this was a compromise between local tradition and preference on one side and the MARC standard on the other.

As the system design progressed, one change seemed to lead to another. Making the 852 repeatable forced us to reconsider notes. The only real place for a location-specific note in the format is in subfield $z in the 852. There is of course no slot in which to put nonbibliographic notes pertaining to the entire run of the serial. We also felt the subfield $z note was too limited for our purposes. We therefore created a nondisplayable subfield $x note, a check-in display subfield $y note, a series of 59x fields to handle general notes, and an 858 field and an 859 field to handle additional location-specific notes.

The holdings format also seemed the logical place to store order, claiming, and binding information for a specific copy of a serial. The USMARC holdings format, being a holdings communication format, quite rightly does not concern itself with this kind of data. We considered appending daughter records to the holdings record, but it seemed simpler to just accommodate the data in the holdings record itself. Therefore we created a series of 95x fields for subscription and fund information (including a link to the source file), a 960 field for claiming control information, and a series of 97x binding data fields. Examples of these fields appear in the holdings record shown in Figure 1 of Appendix B at the end of this paper.

The third type of record, complementing the bibliographic and holdings record, is the *individual issue* record. Its genesis owes much to the kardex. Scribbling notes for posterity on a kardex card is a cherished tradition. The issue record may have started out as an online kardex substitute, but as the system evolved the issue record grew into very much more than that, in effect becoming the center of activity for active serials. The issue record display shows expected issues, received issues, late issues, issues supposed late that are being checked against the shelf or the payfile, issues being claimed, and whatever notes, issue-specific or otherwise, that serials staff wish to make.

The issue records in effect began to assume many of the functions of the holdings format. Next expected issue prediction, for example, is based upon a base issue record (usually the last received) combined with a holdings record 853 definition field rather than on the 853 field plus its latest 863 field.

The issue record's format is modelled on the 853/863 format so that many of the 863 field's subfields have equivalents in issue records. The issue record is very close to being a single issue holdings field, that is, an 863 field containing only one issue. The principal differences are that a single enumeration subfield in the issue record combines a caption and a number and that an issue record contains many extra subfields to accommodate claiming control and claiming history information.

Each issue record has four indicators to supplement the subfields. The first indicates what kind of issue it is (regular, supplement, or index); the second indicates the issue's principal status (expected, late, received, etc.); the third shows a variety of substatuses, and;

and the fourth, for issues that have entered the claiming system, indicates whether or not the system has reported the issue's current status on a written report. A sample issues display appears in Figure 4 of Appendix B of this paper.

Creating the individual issue record to complement the holdings record holdings fields allows the option of bypassing the expansion requirements of the holdings format. Instead of requiring that a compressed holdings field be expandable into individual issues, the system provides the option of actually recording each individual issue in detail. In part, we did this because we thought the holdings statements, if made to reflect all aberrations and changes, would be too complex for public service records, and at the same time would still not contain all the information needed for technical services records. We decided to have the holdings record fields reflect all actual pattern or frequency changes, but not show occasional aberrations from the pattern (for example, an unexpected combined March/April issue). This approach is at odds with the idea of a national, bibliographic-level 853 field.

The system bypasses the *normal* expansion provision of the format. The following description of the check-in system shows that the expansion abilities built into the format's coding are in fact a very important part of the Kansas system.

Automatic and Semi-Automation Check-in

Automatic check-in in the Kansas system is an interaction between a holdings record and its related issue records. There is a "Check-in Display" as such that brings together all expected issues for all copies of a title and allows staff to check-in any or all of each copy's next four expected regular issues, next expected supplement, next expected index, or most recent late or claimed issue. A sample check-in display appears in Figure 3 of Appendix B. All of the real action, however, actually takes place behind the scenes in the holdings records and individual issue records. The issues displayed on the check-in display are just simplified versions of the issue records themselves.

The basic requirements that pushed the development of the check-in system are described below, along with the effects they had on the way the new system does its work and the way the holdings format fits into the total system. The requirements are not in any way unusual.

The first requirement is that to the extent that a serial's publication pattern and numbering are regular, the system should predict the enumeration, chronology, and expected date of the next four expected regular issues, and optionally the next supplement and/or index. As publication patterns change, the expected issues should reflect the changes.

The prediction pattern obviously resides in the holdings record 853, 854, and 855 fields that describe the hierarchy, captions, and publication pattern of a serial. Instead of predicting a new issue based upon the last issue coded within an 86x field in the holdings record, however, the Kansas system bases it on the last received, late, claimed, or missing issue record, or on an issue record specifically designated as a base issue.

The chronology and expected date of the new issues are all based on the frequency in the 853 field subfield $w, modified by any subfield $y coding, as for example: a monthly that skips certain months or publishes an occasional combined issue. The enumeration advances one issue at a time regardless of any subfield coding.

Basing a predicted issue on the last issue record really is in most cases the same process as basing it on the last issue represented in an 863 field. It is more straightforward and, we think, more flexible to base the prediction on a complete issue record, but conceptually it seems to be what the creators of the format had in mind. All the Kansas system does is to use the expansion capabilities of the holdings format to expand beyond the last issue to the next issue. It takes the same pattern that would allow the expansion of a compressed holdings string into individual issues and uses it to predict new issues. It is the same process since what one does in expanding a holdings string is to predict all the individual issues that fit within the string.

The serials department and the planning committee were very concerned that the new system be flexible. The holdings format offers the basis for the flexibility we wanted. It provides for constantly changing captions and publication patterns. For a prediction system to be very flexible, however, not only the pattern but also

112   THE USMARC FORMAT FOR HOLDINGS AND LOCATIONS

the base upon which the pattern operates must be flexible. For that reason, with the one exception of an expected issue especially designated as a base issue, all expected issues for automatic check-in copies are recreated from scratch any time an item is checked-in or the issue record display is updated. The system simply takes the base issue(s) and the information from the proper 853, 854, and 855 fields and creates the issues. Only issue-level notes are retained during the recreation. If the new issues cannot be properly predicted from the old base issues, the user creates new base issues that reflect the new enumeration, chronology, and expected date.

As stated before, the prediction system is based upon the captions and publication pattern coded in the 853/4/5 fields and their equivalent coding in the 853/4/5 fields. It is also based on the expansion capabilities inherent in the coding. Therefore any shortcoming or difficulties in expansion had a large affect on the prediction process.

Predicting enumeration based on subfields $a through $h was reasonably straightforward and easy to implement. The practical matter of programming chronological prediction, however, stimulated three coding changes in the chronology subfields. The format treats chronological levels exactly the same as enumerative levels. Subfields $a through $m of the 853 field, for example, are defined together even though subfields $a through $h treat enumeration and subfields $i though $m treat chronology.

First of all, the four-level principal chronology subfields $i, $j, $k, and $1 did not appear to allow for the completely detailed coding that we desired for daily and weekly-based frequencies, even in combination with subfield $x coding. There appeared to be no easy way to code a span of dates such as "July 6, 1985-Mar. 19, 1986" since each subfield after the first in the string of four gives information relating only to the second half of the coding in the level above it.

The format in one example shows an 853 subfield "i" coded "(date)," allowing complete year-month-day dates to be coded in a single subfield. That approach appeared satisfactory. Therefore we moved the principal chronology from subfields "i" through "1" into a three-part subfield "i," which allows the system to handle complicated dates as well as simpler ones and two-level dates without losing any information and without requiring gymnastic machine calculations. The chronology "July 6, 1985-Mar. 19, 1986" in the Kansas system looks like this:

853 . . . $i (year:month:day) $x 01,07

863 . . . $i 1985:07:06-1986:03:19

This approach works especially well when the dates are very complicated, such as when each issue carries a span of dates, as for example "Jan. 1/13, 1986-March 28/April 10, 1985."

The second chronological coding change is that chronology is always coded as chronology, even if it is the only numbering of any kind to appear on a piece. "May 1985" is thus coded in subfield $i rather than in subfields $a and $b. This makes it much easier for the system to correctly predict issues.

The third change is in the subfield $y exceptions pattern. The Kansas implementation allows a second position definition of week ("w") in addition to the day, month, and season options given in the format. The user can thus code a title that is published weekly except for the last two weeks of the year.

After these coding changes, the last remaining requirement for issue prediction is for there to be links between the pattern 853/4/5 fields in the holdings record and the issue records that relate to them. To create the links the user simply intersperses marker records in the issue record file. The marker consists of the tag (e.g., "853") and the sequence number (e.g., "al") of the holdings field that defines the issues that follow the marker. On the display, that means the issues above the marker. Therefore an issue display for one copy can show a number of markers dividing up the issues. This is very important to the second basic requirement.

The second basic requirement for the check-in and issue update system is that one should be able to check in any current issue and any reasonably recent late, claimed, or missing issue and have the system automatically update the holdings record.

Trying to program the ability to check in automatically any of a number of missing or late issues presented a real problem as long as the program appeared to be one of having an issue in hand, say "vol. 3, no. 5," and trying to determine where in a number of

114   THE USMARC FORMAT FOR HOLDINGS AND LOCATIONS

existing holdings strings it belonged. The logical solution appeared to be to create a holdings record that was completely fluid, in which any update to an issue would reconstruct the holdings statements. The process of turning a group of issue records into a compressed 863 field seemed perfectly proper and logical since the coding in the format was already designed to handle compression and expansion. If the issue records are really just little individual issue holding strings, turning them into compressed holdings statements is exactly what the system should be doing.

Since it soon became clear that this approach probably should not be taken within the entire holdings record, but only within the edge of it that is growing (in our case, the last 852 group of fields), another reason existed to create links between the holdings record 85x fields and their related issue records.

The markers that aid issue prediction provide half of the required link. To hold the entire system together, however, there needed to be again some more content designation in the holdings record. To complete the link, staff must first indicate which 852 group in the record is the active one. Automatic recreation of holdings statements is then limited to that 852 group. In addition, the user then codes the third indicator in 853/4/5 and 863/4/5 field to turn the fields "on" or "off" to automatic recreation. Therefore the system can fit issues in wherever they belong without the necessity that all holdings statements within a group be automatic. It also makes it possible for regular issues to be checked in automatically while supplements and/or indexes are checked in manually. An 853/4/5 field may be turned off, in effect turning off all of the 853/4/5 fields associated with it, or individual 863/4/5 fields may be turned off.

Whenever a check-in or issue update is attempted the system makes sure that there is a marker in the issue records for every turned-on 853/4/5 field in the holdings record, and vice versa. Therefore one set of issue records can contain a number of markers, indicating both different kinds of issues and different publication patterns. All are tied back to the holdings record.

The sample records in Appendix B show an issues display with two 853-field markers, each tied to the holdings record. Each marker defines the issues that appear above it on the display (the issues appear in reverse chronological order, with the latest one at the top).

The third basic requirement of the check-in system is that there should be some alternative to completely automatic prediction and update on one hand, and completely manual updating on the other. The solution to this is something called "semi-automatic" check-in in which the user predicts expected issues, as many or as few as desired, but the system updates holdings record fields just as in automatic check-in. This allows the system to handle some problem frequencies such as semi-monthly and three-times-per-month (at least they are problems for the MARC holdings format), as well as titles with regular numbering but very irregular publishing patterns. It also allows staff to simply record the enumeration and chronology of an issue as it appears and have the holdings record be updated automatically.

CONCLUSIONS

Several conclusions stand out after some reflection on the University of Kansas project. All are based on personal observation and thus are very subjective; none are quantifiable.

The first conclusion is that the *USMARC Format for Holdings and Locations* offers a good basis upon which to build a local serials processing system. It is a good beginning. In particular, the interaction of caption fields and data fields (for example, 853's and 863's) provides a very flexible framework, allowing a single data format and a single pattern of content designation to be presented in a variety of combined formats, both ANSI Z39E and many others. It is a good basic structure.

The second conclusion is that although the format provides a good basis for a local system, it is not sufficient by itself. There are two parts to this. First of all, the format itself needs a little more work to provide for all the items that fall within its assumed communication function, but that do not fit. A holdings format surely should provide the ability to code something as basic as a serial with a semi-monthly frequency. There also need to be more kinds of notes, even in a communications format. The other part is that although the format offers a good beginning, many local processing

116 THE USMARC FORMAT FOR HOLDINGS AND LOCATIONS

systems will want and need places to put much more local data into the record. They will need additional fields, and probably room for more information within several of the already defined fields. This is not necessarily a criticism of the format, but rather a recognition of a difference between intent and function.

The big question is whether the designers of a local system should provide room for more data and content designation by attempting to adapt, modify and add to the holdings format itself, or whether they should design their own format and map elements from it to the national format. Kansas tried the first approach. Now that the project is over, I am not at all sure it was the correct decision. Communicating our holdings will probably be easier because we use most of the format, but there are also added limitations and some loss of flexibility. Our system can't accurately predict semimonthly issues either (at least not yet).

A final conclusion is that it would have been much easier had we not been on the cutting (and bleeding) edge of development. We had no one else's experience to draw upon, no one else's model to copy. We were not working in a vacuum, but the air was a little thin. In contrast, our cataloging system owes much to the many years of online shared cataloging that preceded it. The USMARC bibliographic formats were old friends when we started the cataloging system; the holdings format was a stranger when we began work on the serials system and even now the relationship is not fully developed.

APPENDIX A:
SUMMARY OF THE UNIVERSITY OF KANSAS'
LOCAL ADAPTION
OF THE HOLDINGS FORMAT

A. *Additions to the format.*
   1. Third indicator in all variable fields — used for check-in, claiming, and other local processing.
   2. A variety of 59x and 9xx fields — used for notes, vendor and fund information, binding data, and claiming control data.

3. 858 and 859 notes, functionally equivalent to 852, subfield $z.
4. An 869 field to accommodate negative holdings statements converted from old machine-readable data.
5. Multiple 852 fields (each with a subfield $6 sequence letter) to allow a serial copy divided between two or more locations to be recorded in detail in a single holdings record.
6. A subfield $x nonprinting note in the 852 field.
7. A subfield $y check-in online display note in the 852 field.
8. A subfield $z printing note in the 853, 854, and 855 fields, functionally equivalent to an 863/4/5 subfield $z note.
9. Additional leader data, most notably "check-in type," and an indication of the active 852 group's $6 sequence letter.

B. *Modifications*.
1. The principal chronology is collapsed from subfield $1 - $1 into a three-level subfield $i in fields 853, 854, 855, 863, 864, and 865.
2. Coding of chronology-only materials in subfield $i rather than in subfields $a through $f.
3. Addition of "w" (weekly) pattern to the 853/4/5 subfield $y irregularity pattern.

APPENDIX B:
EXAMPLE OF DIFFERENT DISPLAYS
FOR ONE TITLE

This appendix presents a composite example, displaying the holdings record (Figure 1), reference holdings display (Figure 2), check-in display (Figure 3), and issue records display (Figure 4) for one title (the title is fabricated). The bibliographic record is not shown since it is a fairly standard OCLC-like display, but a few identifying bibliographic fields do display at the top of the holdings record and are displayed on the reference display.

The holdings record display shows a copy divided between two locations (two 852 fields). The principal locations are represented by four-letter codes that are translated on the other displays. Sublocations stored in subfield $c of the 852 field are free-text (none is shown here).

118 THE USMARC FORMAT FOR HOLDINGS AND LOCATIONS

The second 852-group in the record, lines 10-15, is the active one. Its $6 sequence letter "b" matches the "Active 852" code at the top of the record. This 852 group contains two 853 fields reflecting a frequency change from quarterly to monthly. Both the 853 fields and their attendant 863 fields interact with check-in (third indicators are all "1") and their makers can be found on the issues display.

This example shows a title with one holdings record. If there were more than one, the only additional display would be a "Holdings Browse Display" on which the user sees the locations of all copies and then may select the holdings record, reference holdings display, or issues display of any one of them. The reference display is always of one copy only.

John S. Miller 119

APPENDIX

```
                    Holdings Record Display                11/03/86

BIB: 801000015       COPY: 1            Orig: jsm          Mod:
Entered: 110386      Updated: 110386    Check-in type: a   Active 852: b
Mono/serial: y       Status: n          Last C/I: 110386   Appear: y
Rec/acq: 4           Meth/acq: p        Cancel:            Lang: eng
Retn:                Completeness:      Lend pol:          Repro pol:
Ord#: 80-66354-66    Ord date: 090186   Label: y

     1 022        1111-2222
     2 245 0 0    Holdings research review.
     3 260    0   Lawrence, Kan. : $b Office of Information Systems,
University of Kansas, $c 1980-
     4 310        Monthly $b 1986-
     5 321        Quarterly $b 1980-1985
     6 362 0      Vol. 1, no. 1 (spring 1980)-

     7 852 0 0 1  $6 a $a KKU $b KKUA $h Z699.4.M2 $i H67
     8 853 2 0 0  $6 al $a vol. $b no. $u 4 $v r  $i (year:season) $w q $x 21
     9 863 4 0 0  $6 al.1 $a 1-4 $b 1-4 $i 1980:21-1984:24
    10 852 0 0 0  $6 b $a KKU $b KKUK $h Z699.4.M2 $i H67 $y Route to serials
office after check-in
    11 853 2 0 1  $6 bl $a vol. $b no. $u 4 $v r $i (year:season) $w q $x 21
    12 863 4 0 1  $6 bl.1 $a 5 $b 1985:21-1985:24
    13 853 2 0 1  $6 b2 $a vol. $b no. $u 11 $v r $i (year:month) $w m $x 01
$y om12
    14 863 4 0 1  $6 b2.1 $a 6 $b 1-6 $i 1986:01-1986:06 $w g
    15 863 4 0 1  $6 b2.2 $a 6 $b 8-9 $i 1986:08-1986:09
    16 950 1 1 1  FAXON $n 80-66354-66 $o 090186 $s SHIPSD $t 001996
    17 951 1      SO/CSR
    18 952 1      COMSCI
    19 960 1      s $d 3w $n 3
    20 970 1      Hertzberg $b 2455 $c white
    21 971 1      Holdings $a Research $a Review
    22 972 1      s $b c $d 1 $f i $i z $p 3 $s 0 $t 1 $v 1
    23 973 1      KKUA $c KKUK
```

FIGURE 1

120   *THE USMARC FORMAT FOR HOLDINGS AND LOCATIONS*

```
            Copy 1 of 1  --  Reference Holdings  --  Screen 1 of 1

        TITLE:  Holdings research review.
      IMPRINT:  Lawrence, Kan. : Office of Information Systems, University
                of Kansas, 1980-
   FIRST-LAST:  Vol. 1, no. 1 (spring 1980)-
    FREQUENCY:  Quarterly (1980-1985), Monthly (1986-     )
         ISSN:  1111-2222
       STATUS:  currently received (Watson Periodicals)
==============================================================================

     LOCATION:  Watson Stacks
  CALL NUMBER:  Z 699.4 .M2 H67

        vol. 1, no. 1 (spring 1980) - vol. 4, no. 4 (winter 1984)

     ------------

     LOCATION:  Watson Periodicals
  CALL NUMBER:  Z 699.4 .M2 H67

        vol. 5, no. 1 (spring 1985) - vol. 5, no. 4 (winter 1985)
        vol. 6, no. 1 (Jan. 1986) - vol. 6, no. 6 (June 1986)
        vol. 6, no. 8 (Aug. 1986) - vol. 6, no. 9 (Sept. 1986)
```

FIGURE 2

```
                      Check-in Display                      11/03/86

Holdings research review.
    BIB NO: 801000015   REGL: Regular            NO. COPIES: 1
      ISSN: 1111-2222   FREQ: Monthly (1986-)

  1.  Watson Periodicals -- Z 699.4 .M2 H67
        LABEL? Y  INSTR: Automatic check-in -- Route to serials office after
            check-in

        E     10/10/86        vol. 6, no. 10 (Oct. 1986)
        E     11/10/86        vol. 6, no. 11 (Nov. 1986)
        E     01/10/87        vol. 7, no. 1 (Jan. 1987)
        E     02/10/87        vol. 7, no. 2 (Feb. 1987)
        C     07/10/86        vol. 6, no. 7 (July 1986)
```

FIGURE 3

John S. Miller 121

```
                    Individual Issues Display                11/03/86

Holdings research review.
     BIB NO: 801000015   REGL: Regular                NO. COPIES: 1
     ISSN: 1111-2222   FREQ: Monthly (1986-)

     LATEST LOCATION:  Watson Periodicals
         CALL NUMBER:  Z 699.4 .M2 H67
        CHECK-IN TYPE:  automatic         LABEL: Y  LANGUAGE: eng  #ISSUES: 17
        CHECK-IN NOTE:  Route to serials office after check-in

>> . E . . vol. 7 $b no. 2 $i 1987:02 $j Feb. 1987 $r --/--/-- $x 02/10/87
>> . E . . vol. 7 $b no. 1 $i 1987:01 $j Jan. 1987 $r --/--/-- $x 01/10/87
>> . E . . vol. 6 $b no. 11 $i 1986:11 $j Nov. 1986 $r --/--/-- $x 11/10/86
>> . E . . vol. 6 $b no. 10 $i 1986:10 $j Oct. 1986 $r --/--/-- $x 10/10/86
-----------------------------------------------------------------------------
>> . R . . vol. 6 $b no. 9 $i 1986:09 $j Sept. 1986 $r 08/31/86 $x 09/10/86
>> . R . . vol. 6 $b no. 8 $i 1986:08 $j Aug. 1986 $r 08/03/86 $x 08/10/86
>> . C . * vol. 6 $b no. 7 $i 1986:07 $j July 1986 $r --/--/-- $x 07/10/86
             $1 1[LOS1CF](1) 07/29/86 $1 1[POP1CF](1) 08/05/86 $2 143-887
             $3 05/06/86 $4 12.56 $7 7/86-6/87 $8 jsm $9 damag
             $1 1[COCXLT](1) 08/15/86
>> . R . . vol. 6 $b no. 6 $i 1986:06 $j June 1986 $r 06/04/86 $x 06/10/86
>> . R . . vol. 6 $b no. 5 $i 1986:05 $j May 1986 $r 05/01/86 $x 05/10/86
>> . R . . vol. 6 $b no. 4 $i 1986:04 $j April 1986 $r 04/03/86 $x 04/10/86
>> . R . . vol. 6 $b no. 3 $i 1986:03 $j March 1986 $r 03/02/86 $x 03/10/86
>> . R . . vol. 6 $b no. 2 $i 1986:02 $j Feb. 1986 $r 01/31/86 $x 02/10/86
>> . R . . vol. 6 $b no. 1 $i 1986:01 $j Jan. 1986 $r 01/02/86 $x 01/10/86
>> 8 5 3 . b2
>> . R . . vol. 5 $b no. 4 $i 1985:24 $j Winter 1985 $r 12/20/86 $x 12/15/85
>> . R . . vol. 5 $b no. 3 $i 1985:23 $j Fall 1985 $r 09/21/86 $x 09/15/85
>> . R . . vol. 5 $b no. 2 $i 1985:22 $j Summer 1985 $r 07/03/86 $x 06/15/85
>> . R . . vol. 5 $b no. 1 $i 1985:21 $j Spring 1985 $r 03/12/86 $x 03/15/85
>> 8 5 3 . b1
>> 0 0 0 . STOP automatic check-in
```

FIGURE 4

VTLS Serials Control:
Using the *USMARC Format for Holdings and Locations* in an Integrated, Online System

Charles A. Litchfield III
Deborah H. McGrath

On November 1, 1986, VTLS, Inc. delivered a new version of its VTLS software (Release IV.1) to the Virginia Tech Libraries for *beta site* testing. Phase I of the VTLS Serials Control subsystem is a key component of this new software release. VTLS serials control features include check-in and claims records dynamically linked to bibliographic records, automatic anticipation and posting of serial receipts, late issue reminders, claims monitoring, and issue-by-issue updating of holdings records. The mechanism used to link these related records and to enable the automatic serials control processes is the *USMARC Format for Holdings and Locations*.

The organization of VTLS serials control records is depicted in Figure 1, and may enhance the reader's understanding of information presented in this paper.

THE HOLDINGS FORMAT

In developing VTLS Serials Control, design engineers followed the guidelines of the Library of Congress publication *USMARC Format for Holdings and Locations*.[1] The format provides a system-

---

Charles A. Litchfield is User Services Librarian, Virginia Polytechnic Institute and State University Libraries. Deborah H. McGrath is Senior Information Officer, VTLS, Inc.

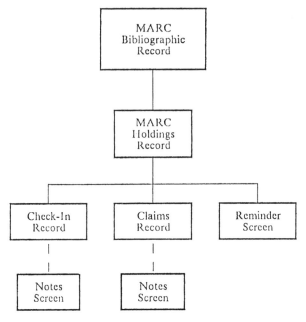

FIGURE 1. Serials Control Data Organization

atic method for recording holdings statements, and use of the format safeguards library data by maintaining those data in accordance with a nationally recognized standard.

The incorporation of all MARC formats into the VTLS software safeguards VTLS libraries' most valuable online resource—their data—and provides reasonable assurance that the data can be manipulated effectively, shared with other library systems that adhere to national standards, and eventually, transported to newer and more powerful systems that may become available.

The VTLS screen image of the coded holdings format (Figure 2) closely resembles the other VTLS MARC record screens. Fixed fields appear in a block at the top of the screen and are labelled. Abbreviations are used as necessary to conserve space (e.g., "Enc lvl" for encoding level, "Acq stat" for acquisition status, etc.).

Four fixed fields not defined by the format have been incorporated for VTLS use. "Local lvl" identifies the method of record entry. For example, the value "4" stands for manual entry, and "5" stands for tape load. "Operator" identifies (in code) the indi-

Charles A. Litchfield III and Deborah H. McGrath 125

```
LIBRARY NAME - - - - - - - - - - - V T L S - - - - - - - - MARC HOLDINGS SCREEN
Local lvl: 4           Operator:      Entrd: 860204   Used: 861119
Type: y   Enc lvl: m   Acq stat: 4    Acq method: p   Lang: eng
Comp: 0   Gen ret: 8   Spec ret:      Com/cop: 0      MBR: 810101
Lend: a   Repro: a     Cancel:        Copies:         UPD:
      004     0313-94760
      035     0033-95430
      090     HV7571.V8 $b Y68
      245 00 Your Virginia state trooper magazine.
      780 02 $t Virginia state policeman
 1.   852     $b 0100
 2.   853 22 6 8 v. $b no. $u 2 $y r $i (year) $j (season) $w f $x 21 $y ps21,23
 3.   854 20 6 8 (year) $b no.
 4.   855     6 1 v. $i (year)
 5.   863 40 6 8.1 2-6 $i 1980-1984 $j 21-23
 6.   863 40 6 8.2 7 $b 1 $i 1985 $j 21 $z (unb.)
 7.   863 40 6 8.3 8 $b 1-2 $i 1986 $j 21-23 $z (unb.)
 8.   864 42 6 8.2 1981 $b 1-2 $z Bound with v. 2
 9.   865    C 1.1 1/5 $i 1979/1983 $z Bound with v. 5
10.   866 30 6 2 v. 1  fall 1979
11.   990    HV $a 7571 $a V8 $a Y68 $a v. $a no.
12.   991    Direct $b 74415
13.   992    Virginia State Police Association (MORE)
             P.O. Box 2189
             8136 Old Keene Mill Road, Suite A-310
             Springfield, Virginia  22152
14.   994    Send dups to Dr. Smith, Criminology Dept.
15.   995    Must claim skipped issues within 90 days.

Please enter NEW COMMAND or 'HELP' for assistance.
```

FIGURE 2. VTLS MARC Holdings Screen

vidual who entered the holdings record. "MBR" stores a bindery record statement and will serve as the link to the Binding Control subsystem scheduled for future development. "UPD" stores a value which determines whether or not check-in transactions are to automatically update the MARC holdings record.

The second portion of the VTLS MARC Holdings Screen contains control numbers and bibliographic data from the MARC bibliographic record to which the holdings record is linked. Data elements include Bib-Id (the VTLS bibliographic record identification number), call number, author, title, and linking entry fields. In accordance with the VTLS design philosophy of avoiding redundant data storage, these bibliographic data elements are called from the MARC bibliographic record for informational display purposes. Should additional bibliographic information be desired, users can access the complete MARC Bibliographic Screen directly from the MARC Holdings Screen.

The third and final portion of the VTLS MARC Holdings Screen

126 THE USMARC FORMAT FOR HOLDINGS AND LOCATIONS

contains the variable fields. Location and copy information, lines of definition, and lines of text are coded into these fields in accordance with the *USMARC Format for Holdings and Locations*. The line numbers in the left column enable modification of tags, indicators, subfield "6" values, and text entries.

While other MARC formats have reserved 9xx fields for local definition and use, no such provision has been made within the MARC holdings format. Since the format makes no other use of 9xx fields, VTLS design staff assumed local use of these fields and employed tags 990 through 995 to store additional data for Check-In and Claims Screens. The 990 field stores marking instructions in repeatable "a" subfields. Source information, source numbers, and acquisition numbers are stored in subfields "a," "b," and "c," respectively, of the 991 field. (NOTE: Source and acquisition numbers serve as links between the Serials Control subsystem and the VTLS Acquisitions and Fund Accounting subsystem.)

Publisher data may be stored in the 992 field, and document numbers (e.g., SUDOCS) may be stored in the 993 field. Fields 994 and 995 can be used to store general notes that appear on Check-In and Claims Screens, respectively.

Data stored in these 99x tags do not appear on the public version of the Holdings Screen and will be suppressed by data output programs to be developed for resource sharing applications (e.g., serials union list production, etc.).

PUBLIC DISPLAY OF HOLDINGS INFORMATION

A key concern for VTLS development staff was formulation of an alternate screen format for displaying holdings data to public access catalog users. Because VTLS is used in a wide variety of libraries, from small public to large academic, a broad range of user capabilities had to be accommodated. Having established the goals of conciseness and ease of understanding, a design group, composed of VTLS, Inc. staff and Virginia Tech librarians, designed the public Holdings Screen.

The Holdings Screen (Figure 3) contains header data and holdings data. The header includes author, title, and call number, which are called from the bibliographic record; location and copy informa-

Charles A. Litchfield III and Deborah H. McGrath 127

```
LIBRARY NAME - - - - - - - - - - - V T L S - - - - - - - - - - HOLDINGS SCREEN

CALL NO : HV7571 V8 Y68
TITLE   : Your Virginia state trooper magazine.
LOCATION: Copy 1 MAIN
STATUS  : Currently received          MBR  1Jan81

v. 1  fall 1979
v. 2-6  spring 1980-fall 1984
v. 7  no. 1  spring 1985 -- (unb.)
v. 8  no. 1-2  spring-fall 1986 -- (unb.)

Supplements:
1981 no. 1-2 -- Bound with v. 3

Indexes:
v. 1/5  1979/1983 -- Bound with v. 5

Please enter NEW COMMAND or 'HELP' for assistance.
```

FIGURE 3. VTLS Public Display Holdings Screen

tion, called from subfields "b" and "t" of the 852 field of the MARC holdings record; and status and MBR statements, called from their respective fixed fields in the MARC holdings record. When the MARC holdings record contains an 843 field (reproduction note), the format statement in subfield "a" also appears in the Holdings Screen header.

Holdings data are divided into the three groups defined by the MARC holdings format: basic bibliographic units (853/863/866 fields), supplements/accompanying material (854/864/867 fields), and indexes (855/865/868 fields). When supplements and/or indexes are present, those groups are clearly labelled on the public version of the Holdings Screen, and the groups are separated by blank lines to enhance readability. Within each group, entries are ordered according to their subfield "6" codes, which (assuming accurate cataloging) equate to chronology of issue.

The goals of clarity and conciseness produced two major differences between the VTLS Holdings Screen and similar screens created by other agencies who have incorporated this format. First, VTLS does not currently provide automatic compression of holdings statements. The design group felt that machine-compressed holdings statements were difficult to read and confusing for public users. An informal study of the 50,000 free-text monographic and serial holdings records in the Virginia Tech Libraries' database

128 *THE USMARC FORMAT FOR HOLDINGS AND LOCATIONS*

early in 1985 revealed an average record length of only three lines. Thus, space was not deemed a sufficient justification for compressing public displays, and the designers chose not to employ compression at this time.

The second difference results from the decision not to algorithmically supply punctuation between data elements. Again, the objective of this decision was to enhance clarity and conciseness of screen images routinely presented to a broad range of users.

Important to note is the fact that the public version of the VTLS Holdings Screen exists only as a screen image. On command, data are pulled from MARC bibliographic and MARC holdings records and formulated for display. Because of this fact, any changes to the Holdings Screen format that may become desirable in the future will require no data manipulation.

LOCAL ENHANCEMENTS FOR PUBLIC DISPLAY

The display capabilities provided by the MARC holdings format enabled VTLS development staff to incorporate a number of local features into the public Holdings Screen. Months and seasons, stored as numeric values in the MARC holdings record, are displayed on the Holdings Screen in the language specified in the "Lang" fixed field of the related MARC bibliographic record. VTLS currently supports sixteen languages:

(cze)	Czechoslovakian	(ita)	Italian
(dan)	Danish	(lat)	Latin
(dut)	Dutch	(nor)	Norwegian
(eng)	English	(pol)	Polish
(fin)	Finnish	(por)	Portuguese
(fre)	French	(rus)	Russian
(ger)	German	(spa)	Spanish
(hun)	Hungarian	(swe)	Swedish

Additional languages can be defined as needed. When the software encounters an undefined language, months and seasons appear in English.

VTLS also takes advantage of the coded entries in the specific retention ("Spec ret") fixed field to provide retention information to public catalog users. The software translates the coded values and displays them as notes on Holdings Screens. The value "12y," for example, appears on the first line of the Holdings Screen as "Library retains only latest 2 years."

Because ordinal numbers are used in issue enumeration for many serial titles, VTLS designers felt that the software should be able to display ordinal numbers on the public Holdings Screen. Ordinal numbers are generated by entering plus characters (+) in 85x fields. Plus signs can be used alone or in combination with print constants. The following example illustrates the use of this facility:

854 20 6 8 $a (year) $b + qtr.
864 40 6 8.1 $a 1983 $b 1-3

Displays as: 1983 1st-3rd qtr.

Issue-specific information stored on "z" subfields of 86x fields also was deemed important for public display. The following example illustrates the use of "z" notes:

854 20 6 8 $a (year) $b + qtr.
864 40 6 8.1 $a 1983 $b 1-3 $z Bound with v. 5

Displays as: 1983 1st-3rd qtr. — Bound with v. 5

HOLDINGS MENU SCREENS

VTLS permits multiple holdings records to be linked to any bibliographic record. This capability allows separate maintenance of individual subscriptions, multivolume sets, etc. The presence of two or more holdings records does, however, require selection of the record to be displayed. VTLS accommodates this selection requirement by formulating and displaying a Holdings Menu Screen (Figure 4).

130 THE USMARC FORMAT FOR HOLDINGS AND LOCATIONS

```
LIBRARY NAME - - - - - - - - - - - V T L S - - - - - - - HOLDINGS MENU SCREEN

CALL NO: HV7571 V8 Y68
   TITLE: Your Virginia state trooper magazine.

   1. MAIN                Copy  1    -Currently received
   2. MAIN                Copy  2    -Currently received
   3. NORTH BRANCH        Copy  3                                Microfilm

Please enter NEW COMMAND or LINE # of selection
```

FIGURE 4. VTLS Holdings Menu Screen

Author, title, and call number information are called from the MARC bibliographic record. Copy-specific data (location, copy number, status, and format) are called from the individual MARC holdings records. Selection of a particular record is accomplished by entering its line number.

CHECK-IN SCREENS

Actual check-in transactions are performed on the Check-In Screen (Figure 5), which is linked to the MARC holdings record. Using the publication pattern established in the last 853 field of the holdings record, the check-in program is able to anticipate expected issues and to automatically update the last 863 field of the holdings record when the expected issue is checked in. When a volume is complete or an issue is skipped, the system automatically creates a new 863 field containing the appropriately coded data. Because these transactions update the database in real time, all users of the online catalog are assured up-to-the-minute information concerning receipts.

The Check-In Screen header contains author, title, and call number called from the MARC bibliographic record, and location, copy number, status, and frequently called from the MARC holdings record. The remaining fields in the header (marking instructions, source information, publisher notes, and general notes) are optional data elements that can be stored in locally defined 99x fields in the MARC holdings record (Figure 6).

Actual check-in data appear in the lower portion of the screen.

Charles A. Litchfield III and Deborah H. McGrath 131

```
LIBRARY NAME - - - - - - - - - - - V T L S - - - - - - HOLDINGS CHECKIN SCREEN

CALL NO : HV7571 V8 Y68                              MARK INSTR
TITLE   : Your Virginia state trooper magazine.     HV
LOCATION: MAIN              Copy  1  -Currently received  7571
FREQ    : Semiannual        DOCS:                    V8
SOURCE  : Direct            SOURCE# 74415    ACQ#    Y68
PUBL    : Virginia State Police Association (MORE)   v.
NOTES   : Send dups to Dr. Smith, Criminology Dept.  no.

        Issue                                    Received  Expected
   1.   v. 5 no. 1 spring 1983                   28Mar83   1May83
   2.   v. 5 no. 2 fall 1983                     27Sep83   1Nov83
   3.   Index v. 1/5 1979/1983                   16Jan84   16Jan84
   4.   v. 6 no. 1 spring 1984                    3Apr84   1May84
   5.   v. 6 no. 2 fall 1984                     15Oct84   1Nov84
   6.   v. 7 no. 1 spring 1985                   26Mar85   3May85
   7. * v. 7 no. 2 fall 1985                               3Nov85 CL
   8.   v. 8 no. 1 spring 1986                   26Mar86   3May86
   9.   v. 8 no. 2 fall 1986                      2Oct86   3Nov86
Expected issue:
  10.   v. 9 no. 1 spring 1987                              4May87
                        Enter 'PS' for more

Please enter NEXT, CK #, CL #, D #, M #, a, REMIND, CL or # * (notes)
```

FIGURE 5. VTLS Check-In Screen

```
  11. 990    HV $a 7571 $a V8 $a Y68 $a v. $a no.
  12. 991    Direct $b 74415
  13. 992    Virginia State Police Association (MORE)
             P. O. Box 2189
             8136 Old Keene Mill Road, Suite A-310
             Springfield, Virginia  22152
  14. 994    Send dups to Dr. Smith, Criminology Dept.
  15. 995    Must claim skipped issues within 90 days.
```

FIGURE 6. Locally Defined Fields

These data can be stored either in coded form (Figure 5, lines 1-2, 4-10) or as free text (Figure 5, line 3).

When a Check-In Screen is accessed, the most recent postings always appear first. The user is, in effect, entering the record at the bottom. The prompt "Enter 'PS' for more" indicates that earlier postings are present and can be viewed if desired. VTLS imposes no limitation on the length of a check-in record. Entries are sorted by "Expected" date.

"Expected" dates are automatically computed and posted for coded issue statements. Computations are based on the previous

132   THE USMARC FORMAT FOR HOLDINGS AND LOCATIONS

"Expected" date and the frequency of publication. Free-text issue statements require manual entry of "Expected" dates.

When the expected issue is checked in, the current date is automatically posted in the "Received" column. When the new receipt has a coded issue statement on the Check-In Screen, the check-in transaction can also automatically add the new entry to the MARC holdings record. Free-text issues must be posted manually to the holdings record.

CLAIMS SCREENS

VTLS Claims Screens (Figure 7) are similar in appearance to Check-In Screens. Header information is again called from the MARC bibliographic and holdings records. Note that separate general notes fields are maintained for Claims Screens (995 field) and Check-In Screens (994 field) (Figure 6). Issues can be posted to the Claims Screen in two ways: 1) transferred from Check-In Screen, or 2) entered as free text on the Claims Screen. When issue statements are transferred from the Claims Screen, the software automatically posts the current date in the "Claimed" column and enters in the "Reclaim" column a date 90 days after the current date. When free-text issue statements are entered, the software automatically posts the "Claimed" date and prompts the user for the "Reclaim" date.

Reclaims are entered from the Claims Screen. A reclaim transaction causes the software to repost the issue statement on a new line

```
LIBRARY NAME - - - - - - - - - - - V T L S - - - - - -  HOLDINGS CLAIMS SCREEN

CALL NO : HV7571 V8 Y68
TITLE   : Your Virginia state trooper magazine.
LOCATION: MAIN                Copy  1  -Currently received
FREQ    : Semiannual
SOURCE  : Direct          SOURCE# 74415      ACQ#
PUBL    : Virginia State Police Association (MORE)
NOTES   : Must claim skipped issues within 90 days.

       Issue                                  Claim #  Claimed  Reclaim
   1. * v. 7 no. 2 fall 1985                            4Jan86   4Apr86
   2.   v. 7 no. 2 fall 1985                    ( 2)    6Apr86   6Jul86

   Please enter D #, M #, A, CL #, REMIND, CK, HM, HS or # * (notes)
```

FIGURE 7. VTLS Claims Screen

with new "Claimed" and "Reclaim" dates. The software also increments the "Claim #" entry by one (Figure 7, line 2).

NOTES SCREENS

VTLS allows up to four lines of free-text notes to be linked to each issue posted on a Check-In or Claims Screen. An issue that has such a note appears on the Check-In or Claims Screen with an asterisk (*) to the left of the issue statement (Figure 5, line 6). Notes Screens can be displayed on command (Figure 8).

REMINDER SCREENS

VTLS alerts technical services staff to follow up on missing issues by generating reminders. Three types of reminders are supported. The software automatically generates a type 1 reminder when an issue is not checked in by its "Expected" date in the check-in record. VTLS automatically generates a type 2 reminder when a claimed issue has not been checked in by its "Reclaim" date. General reminders (type 3) may be entered by technical services staff as needed. One use for a type 3 reminder is to monitor receipt of titles with irregular publication patterns.

VTLS provides two types of Reminder Screens. The general Reminder Screen (Figure 9) contains a listing of all reminders; a spe-

```
LIBRARY NAME - - - - - - - - - - - V T L S - - - - - - - HOLDINGS NOTES SCREEN

CALL NO : HV7571 V8 Y68
TITLE   : Your Virginia state trooper magazine.

7.   v. 7 no. 2 fall 1985                                    3Dec85 CL

   1. Publisher states that a mistake occurred regarding the
   2. number of copies that were published.  It appears that we
   3. were one of the libraries that did not get its copy of the
   4. issue.  Pub. is sorry but has no back issues. (BL 15Mar86)

Please enter D #, D #/#, A # or M #
```

FIGURE 8. VTLS Notes Screen

134 THE USMARC FORMAT FOR HOLDINGS AND LOCATIONS

```
LIBRARY NAME - - - - - - - - - - - V T L S - - - - - HOLDINGS REMINDER SCREEN

      Date      Holding-Id   Type  Remark
  1.  28Jun86   0074-96530    1    Check-in is expected
  2.   6Jul86   0033-95430    2    Claim
  3.  18Jul86   0055-63030    1    Check-in is expected
  4.   1Aug86   0074-32030    1    Check-in is expected
  5.  11Oct86   0059-72930    1    Check-in is expected
  6.  12Oct86   0059-72930    2    Claim
  7.  13Oct86   0069-83930    1    Check-in is expected
  8.  14Oct86   0058-92830    3    Irreg. series -r check receipts
  9.  18Oct86   0055-63030    1    Check-in is expected
 10.  22Oct86   0031-38630    1    Check-in is expected
 11.  26Oct86   0057-33930    1    Check-in is expected
 12.  29Oct86   0009-73230    1    Check-in is expected
 13.  11Nov86   0040-82530    1    Check-in is expected

Please enter D #, M #, A or LINE # of selection
```

FIGURE 9. VTLS General Reminder Screen

cific Reminder Screen (Figure 10) contains a listing of only those reminders associated with a particular holdings record. Reminder Screens are sorted by the dates on which the reminders became due for examination. Additional Reminder Screen data elements include the Holdings-Id (VTLS holdings record identification number) for the issue causing the reminder, the type of reminder, and a "Remarks" field. Line numbers enable direct access to related screens (e.g., Check-In, Claims, Holdings, and MARC Bibliographic Screens).

INTEGRATION OF SERIALS CONTROL WITHIN VTLS

VTLS software design integrates all library data and functions. Access to specific types of data and transaction capabilities are restricted solely by user type as defined during session initiation. The data, transactions, and screen displays developed for serials control have been incorporated into this integrated design.

All types of users can access all but one of the screens described above. Only the Reminder Screens are reserved exclusively for serials processing and management staff. Data manipulation capabilities and check-in and claiming functions also are limited to serials processing and management staff.

The key to integrating the Serials Control subsystem with the rest

```
LIBRARY NAME - - - - - - - - - - - V T L S - - - - -   HOLDINGS REMINDER SCREEN

CALL NO : HV7571 V8 Y68
TITLE   : Your Virginia state trooper magazine.

      Date      Holding-Id  Type  Remark
  1.   6Jul86   0033-95430    2    Claim
  2.   4May87   0033-95430    1    Check-in is expected

Please enter D #, M #, A or LINE # of selection
```

FIGURE 10. VTLS Specific Reminder Screen

of .VTLS was the MARC holdings format. Standardization of the format provided the necessary link for associating the various aspects of serials processing. Storing holdings data in coded form enabled the direct connection between check-in and claiming operations and the public display of holdings statements. VTLS, Inc., regards the *USMARC Format for Holdings and Locations* as a major breakthrough in the management of serials and plans to develop additional automated serials control capabilities, including routing, binding control, and serials union list production.

NOTE

1. *USMARC Format for Holdings and Locations* (Washington: Library of Congress, 1984).

Implementation of the
USMARC Format
for Holdings and Locations
at the University of Florida Libraries

Nancy Lynne Williams

The University of Florida Libraries have had a long history of involvement with serial conversion projects. As early as 1975, Florida was bibliographically converting serials on OCLC for the Florida Union List of Serials (FULS). When funding ended for the FULS project, the University of Florida's Catalog Department was designated as a CONSER participant and FUG began appearing in claimed records on OCLC in 1977. Current cataloging was submitted for CONSER authentication at the Library of Congress and it was not until 1981 that serials retrospective conversion of Florida records began in earnest. In the fall of 1981, the University of Florida, along with the other Southeastern libraries awarded the Department of Education Title II-C grant, began an intensive bibliographic serials conversion project of currently received titles. Most libraries completed the bulk of their conversion over the period of one year. Particularly rewarding to the serials catalogers at Florida was the high percentage of CONSER records available for currently published titles. It was a recognition of the impact CONSER had had on the national bibliographic databases.

While bibliographic conversion was progressing, grant funding was supporting the development of the holdings statement. The

---

Nancy Lynne Williams is Head, Cataloging Department, University of Florida Libraries.

138 THE USMARC FORMAT FOR HOLDINGS AND LOCATIONS

work of the SEARL Holdings Committee is fully described elsewhere in this publication. By the summer of 1982 a draft holdings statement was ready for review and testing. Florida serials and grant staff agreed to be guinea pigs and tried the Format on numerous examples and offered suggestions where further clarification was needed. A second draft was also given a similar test by the University of Kentucky staff.

Florida serials cataloging staff were not again involved with the USMARC Holdings Format until the fall of 1984 when grant funding was received for the implementation of the Format and conversion of holdings information. Florida and Emory University were the first two libraries to begin conversion on SOLINET's LAMBDA system. Emory had been using LAMBDA as an online catalog. Florida was using an integrated system (NOTIS) and because NOTIS had been operational for two years, current serials were being recorded online upon receipt. This provided an opportunity to assess the long range recording of holdings online and to determine the level and amount of detail that would be practical in the ongoing environment.

IMPLEMENTATION

The first month of implementation was especially trying as guidelines and policies were established and staff were trained. A major concern was that all necessary precautions be taken so that later uses of the data in NOTIS would not be jeopardized. Florida was also in the especially limiting situation of being responsible for truly testing the capabilities of the Format. Whenever reasonable the Format's 853s, etc., were fully developed down to the issue level with frequency and publication pattern noted. There was some frustration in having to go to this detail when at the same time receipt statements on NOTIS were summary. For this reason no attempts were made to develop many involved statements for combined issues and/or numerous changes in publication frequency. In some ways it was ironic to work with manual records through 1983 where this detail was obvious from seeing five to ten years of Kardex receipts and then to see summary statements online for 1984 that might read as follows: 1984, no.1-9; or v.4, no.1-4; 1984,

Jan.-Apr. Knowledge of combined issues and frequencies were no longer available. It did raise the question about how important this information is in retrospective holdings as well as current holdings. To test the Format, Florida did develop some holdings statements where there were not too many frequency changes and/or combined numbers.

What has led to a number of rather involved statements, however, has been our policy of creating holdings records that would be complete, i.e., no manual records would need to be consulted for specific issue holdings. The USMARC Holdings record should be capable of being manipulated to provide a public holdings record in the online catalog. For this reason Encoding Level 4 has mostly been used and gaps have been shown. One missing issue has been capable of creating a three or four line holdings statement. The two examples in Figure 1 demonstrate this. The first group is missing the first number of a volume; the second group is missing a number not at the beginning or the end of a volume.

Florida's staffing for the project has equaled one full-time position shared by two half-time professionals for 2 years. Additional hours provided by students and temporary staff have varied from 15

```
853  22  $68$av.$bno.$u12$vr$i(year)$j(month)$wm$x01

863  40  $68.1$a18-20$i1968-1970

863  40  $68.2$a21$b2-12$i1971$j02-12

863  40  $68.3$a22-33$i1972-1983


853  22  $68$av.$bno.$u12$vr$i(year)$j(month)$wm$x01

863  40  $68.1$a18-20$i1968-1970

863  40  $68.2$a21$b1$i1971$j01

863  40  $68.3$a21$b3-12$i1971$j03-12

863  40  $68.4$a22-23$i1972-1983
```

FIGURE 1. Holdings Statements

140   THE USMARC FORMAT FOR HOLDINGS AND LOCATIONS

to 30 extra hours a week. The method used to collect all necessary data was as follows: 1) photocopies of manual Kardex records were made, 2) photocopies were made of the shelf list where bound volumes are recorded, and 3) printouts were made of the copy holdings record on NOTIS. All these items were needed to create one full serials holdings record: Kardex to define the publication pattern and frequency as well as gaps, the shelf list to aid in noting older holdings (missing issues in bound volumes have been noted parenthetically), and the NOTIS records to assist in recording the system's control number down through location and copy number. Working with the NOTIS record was also necessary because many successive bibliographic records were used in converting latest entry manual records. With recording holdings it was necessary to be sure local holdings corresponded with the bibliographic holdings information. The way the control numbers were used are demonstrated in the abbreviated NOTIS record and worksheet segment in Figure 2.

Separate worksheets were prepared for each copy and/or location and future processing will be done on these local control numbers from the 035 and not OCLC numbers and location codes. In fact, the above two locations will be moved into a new Central Science Library in 1987 and this processing on NOTIS control numbers

```
                                    ABS8380
                                    NOTIS COPY HOLDINGS

    Surveying and mapping

    NOTES

    001 2L $a engr $b TA501 $c .A6436
    002 2D $a main,per $b 526.905 $c S963

            Worksheet Example

    035 (NOTIS)ABS8380-001

            Worksheet Example

    035 (NOTIS)ABS8380-002
```

FIGURE 2. Abbreviated NOTIS record and worksheet

could allow location changes to be ignored in matching holding runs.

FCLA AND NOTIS

In 1984, the state of Florida decided that the University of Florida's NOTIS system would be the system for the state's nine universities. The nine universities are: University of Florida, Florida State University, University of South Florida, University of Central Florida, University of West Florida, University of North Florida, Florida A & M University, Florida Atlantic University, and Florida International University. The Florida Center for Library Automation (FCLA) handles all services for the libraries including system development, training, and management. The University of Florida and Florida State University were creating holdings records on LAMBDA as part of the grant and a Holdings Committee of FCLA determined that it would be appropriate to have the other state university libraries also create MARC Holdings records on LAMBDA. In early 1986 the other libraries began work on LAMBDA.

The Format is constructed os that various physical representations of a title can be linked to one bibliographic record. The Florida libraries agreed to consolidate holdings in this fashion; separate holdings records would be created for print and microform representations and would be linked to the bibliographic record that represented the predominant physical format held by the library. In other words, a microform bibliographic record might be used when almost all volumes were microform while the last year or two were paper. Florida has delayed following this procedure until it is certain it will not conflict seriously with the Library of Congress or CONSER guidelines.

One source of frustration for Florida over the last 2 years has been the effort spent on building holdings on LAMBDA and the inability to process the holdings onto the online catalog. Duplication of effort in two separate databases was not desired, so waiting for receipt of LAMBDA's public holdings display record and loading these on NOTIS was and is Florida's general policy. Very recently some brief volume holdings records have been keyed on

142   THE USMARC FORMAT FOR HOLDINGS AND LOCATIONS

NOTIS to provide patron information until the full LAMBDA records can be loaded.

In the fall of 1986 NOTIS's Evanston staff announced plans to program for the use of the USMARC Holdings Format in their system software. A two-phase implementation plan has been proposed that would eventually support the USMARC Holdings formatted record in both a tagged display and a public display. The Florida libraries would like to be test sites for the Format's implementation and using the extensive holdings records keyed into LAMBDA should provide a large database of holdings to manipulate.

The Format accommodates the recording of physical units, but this information more appropriately belongs in the item records that carry bar code, volume enumeration, chronology, and circulation information. A summary command on NOTIS will display all the physical items so bound and physical units with their enumerations and chronology are easily viewed and rearranged in numerical order.

SUMMARY AND RECOMMENDATIONS

Florida librarians have discussed the display of holdings information for public access in our online catalogs. It may be desirable to create a display different from that of the NISO standard; for instance, the display in online catalogs could group enumeration together and group chronology together.

At first reading the *USMARC Format for Holdings and Locations* is forbidding and a little overwhelming. However, as it is worked with, the capabilities and future possibilities of a library's online system provide some guidance in implementing and coding records. As online systems become more complex some of the more specific coding and tagging in the Format may be useful. Catalogers in using OCLC records are accustomed to seeing L, K, and I level records and in some respects these levels correspond to the complexity levels of the Holdings Format. As libraries work with serial holdings, retrospective holdings may carry a more minimal level of detail while current receipts carry the maximum level of detail. Florida is satisfied that its work will be useful in the short run and will be upgradable as integrated systems develop further.

Faxon Serial Interfaces: Implementation of the *USMARC Format for Holdings and Locations* for Serials Check-in and Union List

Mary Ellen Clapper

The purpose of this paper is to examine the *USMARC Holdings Format* as it relates to the automated serial management services offered to libraries by The Faxon Company. The first section provides the background for Faxon's work with the Holdings Format. The issues related to its implementation in the Faxon environment are discussed and the relationship of the Holdings Format with other serial standards is examined. The next section details the implementation and status of the format as part of Faxon's online serials systems, SC-10 and Union List, and Faxon's micro-based check-in software, MicroLinx. The last section explores a series of implementation issues that developed as part of Faxon's work to interface holdings information with a variety of online catalogs, for both locally developed systems as well as other library vendor systems. It addresses the use of the format as a communications vehicle, the issues related to the generation of a holdings display, and presents some alternative methods for storing the data in the communications format. Also presented are additional data elements not currently in the Holdings Format. This data contains relevant serials inventory information that if added to the format may expand its

---

Mary Ellen Clapper formerly Manager, Library/Vendor Interface Services, The Faxon Company, Westwood, MA. She died in May 1988.

144 THE USMARC FORMAT FOR HOLDINGS AND LOCATIONS

uses for circulation, binding, and other interfaces. Finally, a set of issues, with some recommendations for future work on the *US-MARC Holdings Format*, are presented.

BACKGROUND

In 1980, The Faxon Company started its development of a variety of online services to provide a full range of automated serial management services to complement and to interface with Faxon's subscription services. The first service, SC-10, a mainframe computer-based, online check-in system, accessed by institutions using Faxon's LINX network, has expanded from 13 original libraries to the current 140 libraries, representing over 310,000 check-in records.

In 1982, development of the Union List online system was begun in order to provide a system to consolidate individual libraries' holdings into a shared file of title, location, and holdings information representing a group of libraries. An important design feature of the Union List system is to eliminate the need to key holdings information more than once. As a part of the integration of Faxon's online services, libraries using the SC-10 system, and participating in a Union List group, link their check-in records to their Union Lists and the holdings information is automatically transferred.

By 1984, while the size of the files and the number of libraries using Faxon's online services for creating and maintaining their serial location and holdings inventory information was growing, Faxon committed significant development resources to ensure that libraries interested in local control of the serials check-in function would have the option to select a micro-based check-in system, Faxon's MicroLinx. Most important was Faxon's continuing commitment to ensuré that the serials location and holdings information stored and maintained in any of Faxon's automated serials services can be extracted for loading and reporting to a variety of other automated systems. These Interfaces are used to report to automated systems requiring up-to-date serials holdings, e.g., online catalogs, union lists, circulation systems, and regional databases.

Responding to our users' interest and need to interface serial location and holdings information to online catalogs, Faxon made the decision to examine, evaluate, and implement the *USMARC Format for Holdings and Locations* as the communications vehicle for serial location and holdings data from its online systems, SC-10 and Union List, and for MicroLinx. The decision was also made to incorporate the data elements in the Holdings Format into the design and database structure of the MicroLinx system.

Faxon, like other library vendor systems and institutions developing their own local online systems, needed to evaluate how the Holdings Format could be used to enhance the features and functions of its system. At the time Faxon made the decision to implement the format, we were aware that the format itself was still a draft and subject to revision, and that it had not yet been applied in an automated serial check-in environment. Several institutions, many of whose work is also reported in this volume, were developing systems using the format to record detailed serial holdings inventory, namely, retrospective and current summary holdings data. Many of these systems require knowledge of the format in three areas: MARC conventions, which include tags, indicator values, and subfield codes; Holdings language, which includes new terminology, such as publication pattern, captions, enumeration, and chronology; and third, and most importantly, the relationship of individual data elements and fields in order to retrieve and display holdings information, both now and in the future.

Faxon decided to implement the Holdings Format for communication of serials location and holdings data. The purpose is to ensure standard transmission, independent of medium, of up-to-date, accurate location and holdings data in a standard and prescribed format. By selecting a check-in or Union List service that can communicate/exchange data in standard communications format, users of these services are assured of two things:

1. Database building and conversion of serial records relies on a set of standards that will ensure transfer of the data in a standard form, so their serial holdings can be shared in several areas, such as local online catalog and union list reporting.
2. The user maintains the option to migrate to other systems in the future without requiring rekeying of data or writing data conversion programs.

146 THE USMARC FORMAT FOR HOLDINGS AND LOCATIONS

The commitment was made to implement the format in such a way that users would not need to learn the MARC tagging conventions of the Holdings Format or holdings terminology, but would be supported with materials and backup documentation to explain how Faxon's Check-in and Union List systems map to the Holdings Format.

For the SC-10 and Union List systems, this meant evaluating the existing data elements, database structure, and design features in order to understand how we would implement the Holdings Format. Our goal was to develop a behind-the-scenes process so that existing users of the mainframe system could continue their daily check-in and update operations, while extending the use of the same data to other sources. We did not anticipate making major changes to the online system in order to implement the communications format. With SC-10 and Union List, the existing system became the driver of what data could be communicated in the format. This immediately raised issues of what parts of the format could be implemented. For example, in both SC-10 and Union List, summary holdings data is input in a free text field, as the user wishes the data to display. The user controls and selects the display standards they use for their check-in, Union List, and public catalog. It also meant implementing the alternative display feature of the Holdings Format (field 866) for the summary holdings data. Additionally, SC-10 users were interested in identifying and transferring holdings data on the latest issue checked in, missing issues, and bound volume data. This data is also stored ready for display, so a mechanism or convention to identify different types of holdings strings was also required.

Users are also most interested in the relationships of the Holdings Format to the developing, and recently adopted, *American National Standard for Serial Holdings Statements* (ANSI Z39.44-1986), which includes all levels of serials holdings display. The SC-10 and Union List systems leave the choice of the display standard to the user. Several users have established their own guidelines for serial holdings display. There is no clear trend at this time to indicate how much of the new holdings display standard is being used. Libraries not using their own standard do tend to be using the earlier *American National Standard for Serial Holdings Statements at the Summary Level* (ANSI Z39.42-1980).

For MicroLinx, requirements for the USMARC Holdings Format for communication, the ANSI Serial Holdings Statement for display, and the Serial Issue/Article Identification Code were incorporated into the general design. Once again, the Faxon decision was to develop a system with easy to read screens, designed for functionality, and to map the data elements to the Holdings Format. Data entry of tags and subfields is not required. The difference in the implementation between MicroLinx and the already existing systems, SC-10 and Union List, was the ability to incorporate the US-MARC Holdings Format structure in the database design itself, so that data elements are identified uniquely and have corresponding MARC subfields. Based on user requirements and the need to build a system responsive to both the developing USMARC Holdings Format and the *American National Standard for Serial Holdings Statements*, ANSI Z39.44, Faxon implemented four levels of enumeration and four levels of chronology. MicroLinx has a Pattern screen (Figure 1) that prompts the user for publication pattern information that maps directly to the 853 field in the Holdings Format. This screen is also used to determine how the individual check-in item should be displayed. This builds in the option for the user to select the American National Standard Holdings display or the display standard of their choice. Figure 2 illustrates the recording of the same publication pattern information in two different ways: the first using the Standard Holdings display, including prescribed captions and punctuation, the second using a user-defined standard. The resulting displays from the user input are illustrated below the pattern information. Within MicroLinx, display results appear on the check-in screen, the holdings/missing issue screen, and on all the reports. Summary holdings, the HOLDINGS field in Micro-Linx, is actually two fields which display together as a continuous field. The PRIOR HOLDINGS field is used to enter the holdings prior to beginning check-in with MicroLinx. Libraries entering this data are encouraged to adopt the American National Standard for indicating holdings. In a future release of MicroLinx, the system will calculate CURRENT HOLDINGS beginning with the first issue checked in. It will then combine prior and current holdings into the total HOLDINGS field, which displays on all other screens.

The MicroLinx Copy Maintenance screen, showing current expected issue and date (enumeration and chronology data), labels

148 THE USMARC FORMAT FOR HOLDINGS AND LOCATIONS

USMARC HOLDINGS FORMAT FIELDS (853)

PATTERN	LEVEL 1	LEVEL 2	LEVEL 3	LEVEL 4
Label	($a) v.	($b) mo.	($c)	($d)
Alpha, Numeric or Ordinal (use + sign with $a or $b if ordinal number)	N	N		
Continuous Repeating	($v) C	($v) R		
Maximum Number within level		($u) 12		
COVER DATE PATTERN:		Mon ($j)	YEAR ($i)	

Example: [853] 10$61$av.$bno.$ul2vri(year)$j(month)

FIGURE 1. MicroLinx Pattern Screen Map to 853 Field-Publication Pattern

(captions), display punctuation, and the prior and current holdings field is illustrated in Figure 3a. Figure 3b illustrates the "big picture" feature of MicroLinx. Any field with a bar over it is "expandable" — that is, it can hold more information than the space displayed on the screen. A down arrow (↓) at the end of the field line indicates there is more data to be displayed. Also incorporated into MicroLinx, as a part of the predictive check-in function, is the mapping of the individual issue identification elements, i.e., the ISSN, the numbering on the issue (enumeration) and its cover date (chronology) to both the 863 field for enumeration and chronology/subfields in the Holdings Format, and to the draft American National Standard for Serial Issue Identification Code, NISO Subcommittee CC. This feature incorporates bar code scanning of the Serial Issue Identification Code (the SISAC Code) as the method of data entry, rather than keying in a search for the serial item and validating the

Mary Ellen Clapper 149

PATTERN

LEVEL 1		LEVEL 2	LEVEL 3	LEVEL 4
Label	#1	v.;	no.	
	#2	Vol.,	No.	
Alpha,	#1	N	N	
Numeric	#2	N	N	
or Ordinal (use + sign with $a or $b if ordinal number)				
Continuous	#1	C	R	
Repeating	#2	C	R	
Maximum	#1		12	
Number	#2		12	
within level				

COVER DATE PATTERN:

	#1	(Year: Mon)
	#2	Mon YEAR

Example #1:

    [853] 10$61$av.$bno.$u12vri(year)$j(mon)

    [863] b2$6.198700013$7CH$819870301 $a10 $b2$i1987$jFeb.$ov.10:no.2(1987:Feb)

    Display = v.10: no.2 (1987: Feb)

Example #2:

    [853] 10$61$aVol.$bNo.$u12vri(year)$j(mon)

    [863] b2$6.198700014$7CH819870315a10$b3$i1987$jMar.$oVol.10,No.3 Mar.1987

    Display = Vol.10, No.3 Mar.1987

FIGURE 2. Effect of Various Pattern Setup on Holdings Display

predicted issue. An advantage to this type of system design is the ability not only to read data through bar code input, but to generate bar codes identifying the serial issue for use in circulation systems, by its SISAC Code (Code 128) rather than an arbitrary bar coded number. The individual issue identification data elements will also

COPY MAINTENANCE   TITLE#: 732   COPY#   : 2
                                       CHECK-IN SEQ# : 2

Interfaces   TOTAL COPIES : 3
                                       FREQ: BI-MONTHLY

MEDIUM: print   CALL#: HD28.145   LAPSE: 15

ROUTE: yes   CALL# SCHEME: LC

BIND: yes
                                     LIB STATUS: actv 01 Jan 85

CURR SHELF: periodicals   LOCATION ID: DPC   EFFECTIVE :   01 Jan 85

PERM SHELF: stacks   LOCATION: DP Center

SOURCE: Faxon   PRIOR HOLDINGS: v.11,no.3 (June 1971)-v.11, no.6(Dec.1971);V.12(197

	LEVEL 1	LEVEL 2	LEVEL 3	LEVEL 4
LABEL:	v.	:no.		
EXPECTED ENUMERATION:	24	2		
EXPECTED COVER DATE:	01 Apr 84			
EXPECTED RECEIPT DATE:	30 Jan 88			

FIGURE 3a. MicroLinx Copy Maintenance Screen.

PRIOR HOLDINGS
===

v.11,no.3(June 1971)-v.11,no.6(Dec.1971);v.12(1972)-v.20(1980,v21,no.2(Apr.1981),v.22(1982)-v.23(1983)

FIGURE 3b. Example of MicroLinx "Big Picture" on Prior Holdings Field of Copy Maintenance Screen.

be used to generate a claims record using the developing American National Standard for Serial Order, Claims and Acknowledgements. A more detailed description of serial standards and their relationship to each other has been recently published.[1]

IMPLEMENTATION AND STATUS OF THE USMARC HOLDINGS FORMAT IN FAXON'S SERIAL MANAGEMENT SYSTEMS

SC-10 (Mainframe Check-in)

The SC-10 Bibliographic/Holdings Interface turns the user's check-in data in SC-10 into a reusable source of bibliographic and holdings information. This interface allows libraries the option to select the serials check-in system that best meets their technical services requirements, while not limiting their options on their on-line catalog or circulation systems. The objective of the Interface is to output SC-10 location and holdings data for each serial copy in the USMARC Holdings Format on a renewable, yearly subscription basis, at regularly scheduled intervals determined by the user, such as weekly, monthly, etc. This service is presently offered as a tape subscription, but data could be made available via electronic file transfer or on PC diskettes.

Faxon is currently working with several other vendors to effect the interface of serials location and holdings information into an online catalog or MARC editing system using records in the USMARC Holdings Format. This does not necessarily mean that other library system vendors have implemented the Holdings Format. In most instances, vendors are developing a generic holdings loader program that will take Faxon users' data in the Holdings Format and load it into their internal format. However, many library system vendors' development plans do call for future implementation of the Holdings Format. The Faxon option allows libraries to provide the check-in functionality now, while preparing for future options. The key issues for establishing an effective interface using the Holdings Format are:

152 THE USMARC FORMAT FOR HOLDINGS AND LOCATIONS

- linking the holdings records to the bibliographic record in the receiving system,
- agreement on the data elements to be loaded into the receiving system,
- establishing a policy on how microform and hard copy holdings will be reported,
- frequency of reporting,
- consistent generation of the holdings display,
- type of record replacement, i.e., complete file or updates (changes) since the last report, and
- ensuring compatibility of location codes between both systems.

After surveying our user base to determine their needs, Faxon made several decisions related to its implementation of the Holdings Format for SC-10 data. The data elements required by users for transfer of their serial location and holdings data into a receiving system, from the various Faxon systems are outlined in Figure 4. For SC-10, the first step was to categorize the existing data element set and determine which data elements were allied to holdings/location data and thus should be communicated, and which data elements were for strictly local processing and would not be communicated. For both SC-10 and Union List, as will be described below, no publication pattern information existed in the database, since it is not a predictive system. The summary holdings field and the individual check-in issue fields are already in display format.

Several vendors supplying online catalogs are in various stages of implementing a holdings interface with data from Faxon's SC-10 system. A description of these projects follows. It should be noted at this point in the discussion that library vendor systems interfacing with Faxon Serials Check-in Systems need to supply the user with a generic holdings loader program. Generic in two ways, the program will load serial holdings and location data from all three Faxon systems, and the holdings loader does not need to be tailored to each site. In terms of costs for the loader programs, user groups can jointly request this type of generic loader so that development costs are distributed, rather than each site separately negotiating for the development.

Projects to interface SC-10 data with an online catalog have been completed with Brodart and development has begun with Geac, Carlyle, LS/2000, Sperry, and the VTLS systems. The preliminary work to distribute holdings data from SC-10 was developed working with staff from Pennsylvania State University to effect a transfer of SC-10 data into the LIAS system. Although the Pennsylvania State University interface is not completed, the specifications developed for this interface were applicable to the needs of the University of Wyoming, with its decision to implement the Brodart online catalog system. Like Pennsylvania State University, the University of Wyoming is among the five largest SC-10 libraries. They maintain all of their 26,000 serial records online through SC-10 with over 16,000 active check-in terms. User access to serials location and holdings data was provided via a quarterly microfiche product produced by Faxon from the SC-10 system. Technical services staff have access to Faxon's online system, but the Faxon terminals are not in public service areas of the library. With the advent of Wyoming's online catalog, both staff and users identified the need to incorporate serial holdings information in the online catalog. After an exchange of record format, layout, and specifications with the University of Wyoming and Brodart, a one-day working session with all involved parties established a project development schedule and time table. Once decisions on linking, frequency of transfer, location tables, and display elements were agreed upon, Brodart developed the holdings loader. Faxon provided test data from Wyoming's SC-10 file and the technical services staff at Wyoming developed the links between the serial bibliographic record in the online catalog and the copy specific holdings information supplied from the SC-10 system. The Wyoming/Brodart holdings loader established the link using the Faxon title number. The Faxon title number is input into the bibliographic record during the MARC serials record edit process. Most other library vendor systems working with Faxon prefer to have the receiving system's title control number entered in a separate identification field in the Faxon systems. The ability to match in either direction gives the user the option to establish the work flow based on their individual library and systems requirements. Faxon's implementation of the US-MARC Holdings format allows either option.

Libraries selecting an SC-10 interface with their online catalog

Field Name	Description	MARC tag/ position/ field/subfield	SC-10	Union List	MicroLinx
Control number	Unique Faxon record control number; unique user identification record id, specific to the copy level	001	X	X	X
Status codes from Z39.44 Holdings Statement Standard	Receipt/Acquisition Code General Retention Code Completeness Code	008/06 008/12 008/16	X X X	X X X	X
Form of Reproduc-tion code	General material designation	007/00			X
Linkage Control number	Receiving system title control number; user specifies which SC-10 filed to extract from	014	X	X	X
Institution Identifier	User identification number in the Faxon system	852$a	X	X	X
Sublocation codes	User assigned coded location identifiers	852$b (repeatable)	X	X	X
Shelving location		852$c	X	X	X
Location qualifier	indicates temporary location of some issues	852$g	X	X	X

FIGURE 4. Faxon Data Elements Match with Holdings Format Data Elements.

Call number	contains item number as well	852$i	X	X	X
Local form of the title		852$l	X	X	X
Copy number		852$t	X	X	X
Notes	Copy specific notes for display in an online catalog	852$z	X	X	X
Publication pattern for current check-in	includes enumeration and chronology # of bibliographic units, numbering code, frequency (issues per year) regularity and definition date span	853			X
Enumeration and Chronology for individual check-in issues		863			X
Supplements	Enumeration and chronology	864			X
Indexes	Enumeration and chronology				X
Summary Holdings	Alternative holdings display	.866$a	X	X	X
Latest issue checked-in	Display text	.866$b	X		X
Missing issues or not received	Display text	863$c	X		

FIGURE 4 (continued)

156 THE USMARC FORMAT FOR HOLDINGS AND LOCATIONS

must decide what serials holdings data should be displayed for patron access. Most institutions plan to display the summary (compressed) holdings statement, which indicates the extent of the library's holdings, e.g., v.1 (1972)-   . In the online catalog, some libraries may wish to display the most current issue checked-in. Others may elect to show all currently checked-in issues, particularly if the library circulates journals at the issue level. Other libraries may choose to display their missing issues, so that patrons looking for a specific issue will know immediately if it is not held within the library. Faxon's implementation of the Holdings Format for SC-10 provides separate subfields in the 866 to communicate the summary (compressed) holdings statement, the latest issue checked-in, and the missing issues. The SC-10 display screens are illustrated in Figure 5. The matching USMARC Holdings Format field for each data element is next to each field in parentheses. At the present time, Wyoming is not displaying the latest issue received or missing copy information. The Brodart system selects the fields from the Holdings Format based on user-defined requirements.

Before moving to how the same type of Holdings Interface works with Union List and MicroLinx, two issues should be noted. As part of the Bibliographic/Holdings Interface from the SC-10 and Union List systems, it is also possible for the user to receive the bibliographic data for the check-in or union list titles. This is a subset of the data elements that can be found in the MARC serials record. The data provided is sufficient to identify the title as being unique. The objective within the Faxon system is to link the check-in and holdings data to a full bibliographic record that is maintained within the cataloging MARC editing system, not in the serials system. The Bibliographic Interface file is most useful for those libraries who have not yet done MARC cataloging for their serials; or for libraries that have some serial titles in MARC, but not all; or for libraries with the need to provide access to special types of serial materials, e.g., fairly unique items for which MARC records may never become available. This Interface allows libraries to get minimal MARC bibliographic records based on check-in data, so that all serial titles can be represented in the online catalog. These minimal records can be replaced with the full MARC bibliographic record as it becomes available.

Mary Ellen Clapper 157

The other issue to note is the frequency of update. This depends on how much detail the serial holdings display will show in the online catalog. If latest check-in data is included, daily updates are required. At first glance, instantaneous updates would appear to be optimal. Patrons can see the most current issue availability, but may need to wait for some period of time before the issue arrives out of the check-in area into its access location. SC-10 user experience with providing Faxon terminals in public service areas indicates changes must be made to the work flow if instantaneous access is provided.

Union List

Faxon's implementation of the USMARC Holdings Format to distribute Union List holdings information very closely parallels the work done for SC-10. The major difference is the lack of individual check-in issue data or missing issue information. The fields are mapped to the same MARC holdings fields as SC-10. Union List does have more control numbers for linking purposes.

The distribution of Union List data back to a local system from the Faxon mainframe system is a unique application. As most serials librarians are aware, the Union List reporting can be a totally separate reporting process, and may involve rewriting or recording the same data on different forms into different systems, etc. An advantage to the library, by selecting a Union List system that can distribute holdings information in the communications format, is data conversion. Faxon has converted several large existing machine-readable union lists to its online Union List system. Once converted, the holdings data for individual participants is available in a standard format for loading serial holdings information into online catalogs, or building a serials check-in database. Readers may be curious as to why users might select to load holdings from Union List rather than SC-10. In many instances, users decide to maintain all serial holdings in Union List and only active titles within Check-in. Union List data in this case is then the more comprehensive source of holdings data. The Boston Library Consortium was the first and the largest (over 70,000 titles) Union List conversion done by Faxon. The project actually involved two conversions: first, converting the data of the Boston Library Consortium Union

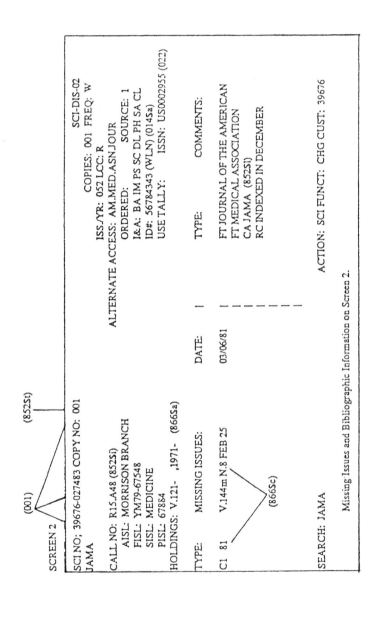

FIGURE 5. SC-10 Check-in Screens Map to the USMARC Holdings Format.

SCREEN 1

SCI NO: 39676-027483   COPY NO: 001
AMA

                                     SCI-DIS-01
                                     COPIES: 001 FREQ: W
                                     ISS./YR: 052 DESC:

    CALL NO: R15.A48   MATRIX: W   ARRIVAL: 014
(852Sb) CURR.ISS: GRADUATE READING ROOM   PUB.STAT: EFF.DATE: 12/03/80
(852Sc) SHELVING: BOUND STACKS, 4TH FLOOR   BINDING: 4 ISS./VOL 12 V/YR TPI: 1
    ROUTING: HARRIS, JACKSON, PETERS   MARKING: GREEN   ISSN: US00029955
    YEAR: 1981   YEAR: 1981

1| V.144, N.1 JAN 7 |01/10/81   14| V.144, N.14 APR 6 |04/09/81
2| V.144, N.2 JAN 14 |01/17/81   15|
3| V.144, N.3 JAN 21 |01/24/81   16|
4| V.144, N.4 JAN 28 |01/31/81   17|
5| V.144, N.5 FEB 4 |02/07/81   18|
6| V.144, N.6 FEB 11 |02/14/81   19| (866Sb)
7| V.144, N.7 FEB 18 |02/21/81   20|
8| *C1* |03/06/81   21|
9| V.144, N.9 MAR 3 |03/06/81   22|
10| V.144, N.10 MAR 10 |03/13/81   23|
11| V.144, N.11 MAR :7 |03/20/81   24|
12| V.144, N.12 MAR :2 |03/27/81   25|
13| V.144, N.13 MAR 31 |04/03/81   26|
YR.COLUMN LINE NO: VOL.NO: STAT.CD: PIECES:
SEARCH: JAMA   ACTION: SCI FUNCT: CHG CUST: 39676

Check-in and Bibliographic Information on Screen 1

FIGURE 5 (continued)

160 THE USMARC FORMAT FOR HOLDINGS AND LOCATIONS

List and then the conversion and merger with the Massachusetts Institute of Technology's serial list of over 20,000 serial titles. This merged Boston Library Consortium Union List is currently available online for maintenance, and in a variety of microfiche products distributed by the consortium office. Additionally, several individual member institutions produce their own microfiche or printed list. With the implementation of the Holdings Interface, union list libraries are also able to receive their holdings data on an ongoing basis to update their online catalogs. MIT worked with Faxon and Geac to load their serial holdings data into the Geac MARC editing system in order to make their serial title and holdings information available through their Geac system. Using this development as a prototype, Faxon and Geac have begun the work to provide a generic holdings loader that will allow libraries using SC-10, Union List, or MicroLinx to update their serial holdings automatically between the two systems. A separate development is underway with Boston University, one of the initial SC-10 libraries, and a member of the Boston Library Consortium. Boston University has recently installed the Carlyle system for its online catalog, while continuing its use of SC-10. An interface between the Carlyle system and holdings data from Faxon's systems, SC-10, Union List, and MicroLinx is currently being developed.

For the Holdings Interfaces discussed so far, the exchange of holdings data using the Holdings Format is geared to the exchange of holdings data already in display format. The initial implementation of the Holdings Interface with Geac, LS/2000, Carlyle, and Brodart uses the alternate holdings display (field 866) data. Preliminary discussions with other library vendor systems, namely, DRA and Dynix, also involve the exchange of display text for holdings data. These receiving systems do not presently have the capability of generating displays from enumeration and chronology fields (863s), nor do they support the publication pattern field (853). Eventually, i.e., when the vendors are more sure of the stability of the format and users require its support as part of their functional specifications, I expect that more systems in the future will be able to generate displays from the more detailed data that can be communicated by the Holdings Format.

Faxon changes to the format, or local adaption to use the format to deliver the users' requirements were carefully considered. For SC-10 and Union List files, the location information is distributed in field 852, and field 866 is used to distribute the holdings. Compression and expansion, that is, the ability of detailed level holdings to be compressed into summary level holdings, and summary holdings to be expanded into detailed level holdings statements, is not part of the implementation.

It was clear from our users and the vendor systems with whom we are creating interfaces that it would be necessary to distinguish among the summary holdings statements, the latest issue checked in and the missing issues. We saw two options: to put each string in a separate 866 and add some type of subfield identifier to indicate the type of holdings information being transferred or to define additional repeatable subfields in the 866 to define the checked-in issues in display format (either all issues or just the last issue) and to describe a field for missing issues, should the online catalog system (receiving system) wish to display this data to its users.

We are in the process of implementing the second option for SC-10. The Holdings Format makes provision using the indicators of 863 in combination with 866 to identify which field to use for display. The provision to differentiate the summary (compressed) holdings from the individual details items in the indicators of the 863. We saw no reason to use the 863 if the same information could be incorporated into the 866. Unfortunately, the 866's first indicator details the level of specificity. This is the same as the 863's 1st indicator use. But the 2nd indicator for the 863 defines compressed or uncompressed single items and in the 866 it defines standard or nonstandard display information. Since Faxon's implementation is driven from the check-in side, at this point we wish to ensure that the receiving system can identify and select those holdings strings it wishes to display.

So for the present, for SC-10, instead of changing indicator values in the 853 or 863, we opted to implement an alternate display subfield b ($b) for the single item, last check-in issue. Subfield c ($c) is used for missing issue fields. We would propose a change to the format that makes the indicator values in the 853/863/866 carry the same type of information and create a subfield within the 863/866 to define the type of display notation scheme to be used. More

162   THE USMARC FORMAT FOR HOLDINGS AND LOCATIONS

discussion on the issue of matching up content designated (i.e., full use of the 863 field) check-in item information for each specific issue, with a display version for each specific issue, is addressed in the MicroLinx section that follows.

With the work we are doing with system interfaces, it is presently a requirement that holdings data, ready for display, is the form preferred by most receiving systems for receiving data. Online catalog systems, for the most part, are willing to let the check-in side of the operation generate the display. At Faxon, we are presently providing the display option for SC-10 and Union List, and both options, i.e., display or full content designation, with MicroLinx.

MicroLinx

The implementation of the USMARC Holdings Format during the design and development of MicroLinx was much more challenging than its implementation with the online systems, SC-10 and Union List. Within the MicroLinx system, the relationship of the publication pattern (853) to the summary holdings (866) and to the individual check-in items (863) has been established, as well as the rules and guidelines for implementing the Holdings Format without requiring tag and subfield input. Faxon has been fortunate to be able to work with the University of Georgia in the implementation of the format. The University of Georgia has developed its own local online system, MARVEL. A discussion of the implementation of the Holdings Format and manipulation of data for holdings display at Georgia also appears in this volume. Building on the work done at the University of Georgia to input data via holdings format screens and to generate displays of holdings data, the University of Georgia/Faxon project seeks to define how to replace holdings data entry with check-in information as it is entered into the MicroLinx system. The MicroLinx to MARVEL interface is accomplished using the MicroLinx Holdings Interface utility. The Holdings Interface software extracts holdings information from MicroLinx for transfer to MARVEL.

MicroLinx software, including the Holdings Interface utility, operates on the IBM-PC/AT and compatibles. The Holdings Interface outputs a PC/DOS file of holdings records in the USMARC Holdings Format. This file can be transferred to the mainframe (host computer) through a simple RS-232 serial port connection. The publication pattern data is the key to compressing or expanding holdings information once it is stored in the USMARC Holdings Format. Where the publication pattern data resides is a function of how holdings displays are generated. As mentioned above, Faxon is attempting to provide maximum flexibility in terms of how the holdings data is transferred, so that interfaces are possible with systems expecting data ready for display, and with those that will generate displays from 853/863/866 combinations. For systems that are using data stored in the communications format to generate holdings displays, access to the full history of the publication pattern, or the history of the publication pattern as far back as the library has recorded holdings, is a requirement. Within the predictive check-in environment, it is required to know the current pattern, and to issue an alert within the system when it changes. This alert acknowledges the pattern change, creates a new 853, closes out the date range for the earlier pattern, and starts a new date range for the new 853 field.

Intrinsic in the design of the MicroLinx Holdings Interface is its automatic reporting of up-to-date or latest information about the status of each individual issue for each copy. In order to take full advantage of the 853/863 information, it assumes that the day to day check-in operation will be used to update the compressed summary holdings data. It assumes that the publication pattern information will be maintained in a larger database, and that the system generating the holdings display will update the 863 fields as necessary. MicroLinx will keep track of the latest publication pattern field.

A brief description of the MARVEL/MicroLinx interface follows. The MARVEL system receives a sequential file of MicroLinx holdings records, based on the parameters selected at the time the Holdings Interface utility is run. The receiving system matches and links the individual issue level record information to the correct copy record in the MARVEL system. The linking is based on a combination of the MARVEL system control number and fund codes. This information is stored within MicroLinx and passed to the receiving system in the Holdings Format. The next step in the match is the comparison of the pattern information. The system

164 THE USMARC FORMAT FOR HOLDINGS AND LOCATIONS

looks for an exact match, which indicates the incoming check-in issue information continues to match the existing publication pattern data stored in the most current 853 in the MARVEL system. The sequence control numbers in subfield 6 ($6) are maintained in the receiving system. MicroLinx does not assign a sequence control number for the 853, or maintain an ongoing sequence control number. The default value in the 853, passed to the receiving system, is always "1." Once the MARVEL system verifies the exact match, the 863 field is updated, compression occurs, and the new holdings display field is generated.

The MicroLinx Holdings Interface outputs holdings data according to the hierarchical levels of holdings maintained within MicroLinx itself. MicroLinx stores all title information together, so that all bibliographic information [namely, linking entries, alternative forms of access, subject entries, and most importantly for linking purposes, the linkage control number (field 014), which defines the title control number in the receiving system] is stored at the title level in MicroLinx. This feature enables the library to report holdings of various types (e.g., microforms) all to the same bibliographic record in the online catalog. The next hierarchical level in MicroLinx is copy level information. At this level, information specific to a particular copy, such as the type of microform received, is stored. This feature enables the user to establish different check-in patterns based on the type of media in which the material is received. Those who have handled microform receipt recognize the need for very different check-in patterns than for the hard copy issues. The last and most detailed hierarchical level for MicroLinx is the issue information. This data which is output in the 863 field represents a wealth of information to be sent to the receiving systems. A design criterion was to keep all the information related to one issue together and in the correct sequence. Trying to keep track of both the display version of the issue information in the 866 while at the same time keeping track of the individual issues within the 863, represented a challenge to maintaining the sequence numbers correctly, and also represented a significant duplication of data by requiring the content designated version to be stored in the 863 and the display version to be stored in the 866, while setting the appropriate indicators.

Another factor that entered into our implementation decision was how and where to record additional detail related to a specific issue. Detail information for monographic series, such as the author, title, ISBN, and call number, was requested with sufficient frequency by our users so that the decision was made to provide the data, when available, as part of the subfields related to a specific issue. This necessitated defining more subfields within the 863 than are provided by the existing format. An argument for not adding more subfields is to establish the link from the specific issue back to a separate bibliographic record. An example of this type of linking would be an analyzed series that is separately classified. Both the bibliographic record for the serial as well as individual bibliographic records for each item could exist in the catalog database. How to link these records, and more importantly, how to generate a "helpful" holdings display for the patron requires complex design and programming. In its initial implementation, we have defined four additional subfields ($u, $v, $w, $x) in the 863 to communicate author, title, call number, and ISBN for a specific issue within a serial, should they be available and assigned. It was unclear to us how the 863 subfield s ($s) was intended to be used. As defined, this subfield contains the unique identification code for component parts appearing in monographs and serials. Although repeatable, it does not uniquely identify the data that can be associated with the title of a specific issue. We were also not sure that its intended use matched the need we are trying to fulfill by passing issue-specific information to the receiving system.

The third and final requirement that Faxon identified in providing check-in data to a more generalized holdings system for generation of compressed displays, is identifying the status of an issue-specific item at any particular point in time. The important point in time is "the users." How to alert the user that a specific issue is checked-in but is being routed through the library, or is someplace in the claiming or binding process? MicroLinx tracks the status of every issue by maintaining a set of status codes and their associated dates. A list of the MicroLinx status codes is found in Figure 6. Communicating the status and date is an important element for holdings display if information on claimed or bound issues is to be provided. As part of the MicroLinx implementation of the Holdings Format, a set of

166 THE USMARC FORMAT FOR HOLDINGS AND LOCATIONS

CODE	DESCRIPTION
CH	Check in an issue.
NR	Issue not received.
UN	Undo action.
C1	First claim request.
BP	Issue being prepared for shipment to the bindery.
BI	Issue has been bound (returned from bindery).
DY	Issue is delayed.
MS	Issue missing - e.g., has been lost since check-in.
NO	Not ordered.
NP	Not published.
OP	Out of print.
WL	Want list.

FIGURE 6. MicroLinx Action Codes: Check-in Actions.

repeatable subfields, $7 and $8, have been defined. Subfield 7 ($7) supplies the action code, and subfield 8 ($8), supplies the date of the action. Earlier or previous actions are provided in the same repeatable subfields. The most recent action appears first.

The sequence control number provided by MicroLinx in subfield 6 ($6) of the 863 is a combination of the date and the line number as a decimal point after the default sequence control number of 1. MicroLinx uses the same conventions and additional subfields to describe supplements in the 864 field and indexes in the 865 field.

After weighing the requirements for fully content designated, issue-specific data for each item checked-in, as well as providing its display version, the following compromise has been implemented within MicroLinx. Summary (compressed) holdings statements are recorded in the PRIOR HOLDINGS field. The data in this field is output in the first 866 field. Issue-specific data from check-in is output in the 863 field and the display version appears in subfield o ($o). For receiving systems that are only picking up display holdings for the latest issue checked-in, the last check-in issue in its display format also appears in the 866 subfield b ($b). This maintains consistency with the data coming from SC-10.

Faxon's implementation of the format at the check-in level raised many issues. In the preceding paragraphs, I have attempted to describe our proposed solutions and have explained the changes we have made or new fields that have been added to allow us to implement the Holdings Format while maintaining flexibility. It is our plan to always sequence the summary (compressed) holdings as the first item in the 866. Faxon users have also expressed interest in interfacing their serials data, either SC-10 or MicroLinx, with additional vendor systems that are also implementing the Holdings Format. Both NOTIS and VTLS implementations are of interest to Faxon LINX users. Both implementations will allow the loading of holdings data from other sources, provided the data is in the USMARC Holdings Format. As required by our users, test and then production loads of data from the Faxon systems into these other systems will be arranged.

CONCLUSIONS, RECOMMENDATIONS, AND FUTURE ISSUES

During the MARBI meetings at the 1987 American Library Association San Francisco Conference, the USMARC Holdings Format will be reviewed. Implementors, like Faxon and other vendors and institutions whose work appears in these pages, will be sharing their experiences with the Format, and discussing additions, changes, and suggested new fields or enhancements. As more vendors gain experience with the Format, the Format takes on a life of its own. The good news, as already demonstrated, is that the Format is currently working extremely well as a standard for communications and exchange of the holdings data. It is important to emphasize that it is a standard for communicating the data and it does NOT mean that local or vendor applications MUST use MARC tagging to define fields for input.

I have tried to focus on the implementation of the format in a serials control environment. Faxon's work confirms that the format adequately defines the data elements needed to describe the publica-

168 THE USMARC FORMAT FOR HOLDINGS AND LOCATIONS

tion pattern, in order to identify the next predicted serial issue. The format makes provision for the coded values associated with an individual copy of a serial. These values are defined as part of the ANSI Z39.44-1986 standard for Serial Holdings Statements. The Holdings Format documentation explains and provides for the enumeration (numbering) and chronology (dates), for alternative numbering schemes, and for the captions (labels) that appear on each specific issue. It has adequate provision for the handling of supplements and indexes, explains how to identify gaps, and sets up subfields for recording frequency, continuous and restart numbering, issues per year, calendar changes, and hierarchical levels for numbering. Rules are established that apply to predictive check-in, claiming, binding, and compression of holdings. We think that adequate provision has been made to distinguish between logical bibliographic units and physical units.

Faxon's established goals for the implementation of the Holdings Format for check-in included:

- to transmit data according to the Format,
- to require minimal machine time to process the check-in operation and update holdings,
- to avoid tagging and content designation whenever possible,
- to support the Serial Holdings Statement display formats at all levels,
- to transmit either fully content designated data or holdings already in display format,
- to allow the system to handle punctuation of the holdings strings, whenever possible,
- to support compression of summary holdings statements, punctuated and displayed according to the Serial Holdings Statement standard, and
- to provide single keying at check-in time, i.e., enter the data once and the system handles check-in, inventory control, and summarized (compressed) holdings.

After establishing these goals, we next examined how the format could be implemented and used for serials control. We identified a series of design decisions and features that would need to be answered as part of our implementation:

- How do other systems use the Format and how can interfaces be achieved?
- For the required functionality, does the system require all of the data elements defined by the Format, or are others required?
- Can the required data elements be mapped to the Format?
- How are the coded values entered and displayed?
- How much MARC tagging is required?
- How easy is the system to use; how much staff training is required for efficient data entry?

We also evaluated the processing requirements:

- How does compression work?
- What is needed for expansion?
- What display rules should be followed?
- Are there separate technical services and public access display screens?
- What will be seen by the user?
- Does the system generate the public access display in real time, or is a display version stored separately?

For others planning to implement the Holdings Format, I have listed a set of decisions you face:

- How will you implement the Format — for communication, for data entry, for technical services displays, for all of the above?
- Can the system receive and output data in the Holdings Format?
- How and where will the publication pattern fields be generated and maintained?
- Will the system maintain a complete inventory of holdings data?
- What determines the starting point for holdings? For check-in?
- Where should publication pattern data really reside? Is it really bibliographic?
- What information is required for a predictive check-in system?

170 THE USMARC FORMAT FOR HOLDINGS AND LOCATIONS

Current publication pattern? How will pattern changes be identified?
- How are sequence control numbers assigned, maintained, and kept in order?

Beyond the scope of a single institution or vendor implementation, there are some additional issues related to the USMARC Holdings Format that need to be addressed in a larger forum. My purpose is to raise the questions and encourage a continuing dialogue among all those seeking to facilitate and streamline the identification of serial holdings. The first of these is the storage, maintenance, and distribution of publication pattern data. I raised the question earlier. If this data is really bibliographic, should it be associated with a serials bibliographic record? A national database of publication pattern information, associated with serial titles and available for distribution, would certainly speed the process of creating serial holdings inventory records. It is staggering to think of the repetitious data entry of 853 fields that may be proliferating as serial holdings databases are created. A project similar to the CON-SER Abstracting and Indexing Project could oversee the creation of such a database and establish the rules and guidelines for its maintenance. Serial subscription agencies should be encouraged to be participants in such a database, since the currency of their information is most useful to the libraries at check-in. In addition to the creation of this type of database, the issue of which MARC Format should carry the publication pattern data should be addressed by the Library of Congress in the near future. Even if the current structure is not changed, an evaluation of the issues is warranted. A clearer sense of the direction of the Format should be the result of such an evaluation.

Another outstanding issue is the relationship of the ANSI Z39.44-1986 Serial Holdings Statements standard and the US-MARC Holdings Format. This new standard details the guidelines for generating serial holdings displays. While the Holdings Format is independent of the display, the rules for compression make it much simpler to generate a holdings display that separates the enumeration from the chronology, e.g., v.1-v.10 1971-1980, than to generate a summary (compressed) holdings statement that keeps them together, e.g., v.1 (1971) -v.10 (1980). The reality for vendors responding to proposals will be the requirement both to implement the communications format and to be able to generate holdings displays according to the holdings display standard. From my perspective, this issue is further complicated when the recording of retrospective holdings information is tied into an automated check-in system. It is most natural for the individual issue holdings display to follow the new standard, e.g., v.11: no.2 (1981: Feb), keeping enumeration and chronology together. Compressed holdings strings that separate enumeration from chronology then appear different to the patron. As part of the review of the format, my suggestion would be further discussion among the implementors about ways to generate the holdings statements to match the holdings display standard. Information on the features and development of the new standard are to be found in the paper by Marjorie Bloss in this volume. In addition, an article by Bloss in the Winter 1987 issue of *Library Resources and Technical Services* describes the features of the new standard and explains the differences from the earlier standard.[2]

I would also like to see the issue of redundancy of storing the publication pattern data (field 853) in each local record addressed. I'd like to hear of other implementations that provided a solution, so that the same data is not repeated in each local holdings record.

The last issue I raise is one of the communication transaction itself. Is the communication of a holdings record being used to communicate the latest transaction that indicates what's been added or changed; or is it meant to store the complete history of the holdings for that particular copy; or in some applications, is it doing both? From my perspective, it would appear that the earliest implementations of the Holdings Format are meant to contain the complete history. I would like to suggest a scenario that shows that once retrospective conversion on serial holdings has been completed, the Holdings Format could be used to communicate a transaction but would not involve sending the entire holdings record. Will some provision for these holdings transactions be made in the future?

The short term indicates that the USMARC Holdings Format is

172 THE USMARC FORMAT FOR HOLDINGS AND LOCATIONS

viable, and is being implemented as systems develop and add enhancements. The long term indicates that a continuing dialogue among all interested parties needs to be promoted and encouraged. I look forward to revisiting these issues in the future.

NOTES

1. Mary Ellen Clapper, "Standards for Serials." *Serials Review* 12, no.2/3 (1987): 119-131.

2. Marjorie E. Bloss, "The New! The Improved! Standard for Serial Holdings Statements." *Library Resources & Technical Services* 31 (Jan./Mar. 1987): 24-34.

The NOTIS Implementation of the *USMARC Format for Holdings and Locations*

Peggy Steele

The development of the *USMARC Format for Holdings and Locations* has opened up many exciting opportunities for controlling and using holdings data in automated library systems and for communicating and sharing holdings data among individual libraries, library consortia, and bibliographic utilities. Although the US-MARC Formats are primarily communications specifications designed to facilitate the transmission of data from one computer system to another, they have also had a tremendous influence on the way that bibliographic and authority data is handled locally within individual systems. This is not an insignificant benefit to the library community as it promotes a certain level of consistency in thinking about what kinds of data are important to libraries and to their users, why the data is important, and how we should best utilize it.

The value of nationally accepted standards like the MARC Formats, and also the NISO standards for serial and nonserial holdings, is sometimes reflected most clearly in their absence, as is surely the case with the Holdings Format. The previous lack of standardization in this area has prevented, or at least has made exceedingly difficult, the communication of much important information among libraries in the United States. Lacking guidance for location and holdings data at the national level, the individual utilities, library systems, and libraries in the United States have developed their own

---

Peggy Steele is Systems Analyst, NOTIS Office, Northwestern University Library.

guidelines and conventions for handling this data or, as is probably true in many cases, adopted a variety of conventions over time. The advent of the *USMARC Format for Holdings and Locations* and the NISO standards at last provides a framework for dealing with holdings and location data in a systematic way.

NOTIS is a MARC-based system with a long-time commitment to supporting all the USMARC Formats. Although we have long had a concise and systematic mechanism for internally handling both locations and holdings, we have looked forward with much enthusiasm to the release of the Holdings Format for the opportunity it would give us to review and standardize our practices, particularly in the area of holdings. In mid-1986, we undertook a major development project to incorporate the Format, also known as MFHL (pronounced affectionately as "muffle" by the NOTIS staff) into our system. We anticipated the benefits of this project to be manifold, enabling NOTIS not only to store and share holdings information in a standardized form, but also to build many enhancements to our system using a new Format-based holdings record as a foundation.

NOTIS RECORD STRUCTURE

To see how the Holdings Format fits into the total picture at NOTIS, it is important to have a basic understanding of the system and its record structure. From the very beginning, NOTIS was intended to be a comprehensive and flexible integrated system for managing library materials of all types and for providing online public access to all of the materials in a library's collections. The basic architecture of the system, as seen by library staff, is shown in Figure 1. The architecture embodies the principles of integration and nonredundant data storage and allows the system to serve the needs of both library staff and library patrons through use of one comprehensive database.

The most important component of the NOTIS architecture is the MARC bibliographic record which serves as the foundation of the record structure. An example of a NOTIS bibliographic record for a serial publication is shown in Figure 2. NOTIS supports all existing USMARC Formats for bibliographic data and consequently can be

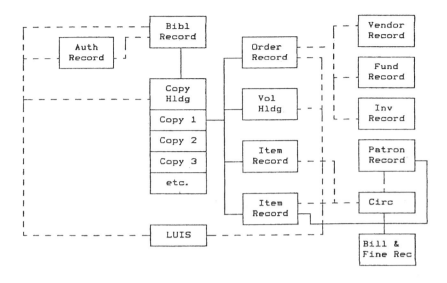

Solid lines represent permanent links between records.

Broken lines represent temporary relationships that can exist between different types of records.

FIGURE 1. NOTIS Record Structure

used to control all types of library materials. NOTIS utilizes NOTIS/MARC, a display version of USMARC that is easily learned and recognized by library staff.

A basic feature of the NOTIS system design is that the bibliographic record contains only bibliographic data. Any local information, such as the call number and location of a specific item, is stored separately in a copy holdings record that is linked to the bibliographic record. A typical copy holdings record for a serial may be seen in Figure 3. The copy holdings record contains one copy statement for each copy the library wishes to control through the system. Each copy statement contains location and call number data for one copy as well as coded processing status information (fully processed, on-order, in process, withdrawn, etc.) and other kinds of copy-specific data. For each copy there are three other types of records that may exist in the system:

176 THE USMARC FORMAT FOR HOLDINGS AND LOCATIONS

```
LTNU DONE                                              ACS9292
                                        NOTIS CATALOGING      L4XB
NU# ACS9292 FMT S RT a BL s DT 11/29/83 R/DT 05/17/84 STAT MM E/LEV DCF a
SRC d PLACE nyu LANG eng MOD   OA a REPRO   S/STAT c DT/1 1983 DT/2 9999
CONT     S/T p FREQ q REG r MED   GOVT   TPA   IA   CIA ? ISDS   CONF 0 SLE 0

010:  : $a sn 82002028
022/1:0 : $a 0731-7131
035/1:  : $a (OCoLC)8234865
040:  : $a NSDP $d IEN
042:  : $a nsdp
222:00: $a Technical services quarterly
245:00: $a Technical services quarterly.
260:00: $a New York, N.Y. : $b Haworth Press, $c 1983-
265:  : $a Haworth Press, 28 E. 22nd St., New York, N.Y. 10010
300:  : $a v. ; $c 22 cm.
320:  : $a ivpy $b 4/1
350:  : $a $75.00 (U.S.) $a $85.00 (individual, foreign) $a $95.00
(institution, foreign) $a $105.00 (library, foreign)
362/1:0 : $a Vol. 1, no. 1/2 (fall/winter 1983)-
650/1: 0: $a Library science $x Periodicals.
650/2: 0: $a Library science $x Technological innovations $x Periodicals.
650/3: 0: $a Libraries $x Automation $x Periodicals.
```

FIGURE 2. NOTIS/MARC Bibliographic Record for a Serial

```
LTNU DONE                                              ACS9292
                                      NOTIS COPY HOLDINGS      L4XB
 NU SERL LC sn 82002028   ISSN 0731-7131 S/STAT c FREQ q S/T p CFR 4/1
Technical services quarterly. Vol. 1, no. 1/2 (fall/winter 1983)-      -- New
   York, N.Y. : Haworth Press, 1983- Haworth Press, 28 E. 22nd St., New York,
   N.Y. 10010
 STATUS h DT 04/30/84 AD none
 NOTES $a p:MMK
 001 2D CN $a main $b 020.5 $c T255 $v v.                         $d 11/29/83
    NOTES $a ci:pr
    ITEM RECORDS      1
    A-001-001
```

FIGURE 3. NOTIS Copy Holdings Record

- volume holdings records
- item records
- order/pay/receipt records

One volume holdings record can be linked to each copy statement. The volume holdings record is essentially a free-text storage area that can be used to record detailed or summarized statements of the volumes owned by the library. An example of a NOTIS volume holdings record using a set of holdings conventions defined locally by Northwestern University Library in the mid-1970s is shown in

Figure 4. It is possible to record data here in any format chosen by the local library.

There can be one or more item records linked to each copy statement. Each item record represents a physical piece owned by the library and contains the item's barcode number or other unique identifier along with several other pieces of information that are essential for automated circulation and inventory control. Whenever an item is charged to a patron in the NOTIS circulation system, the charge data is stored in the item record. A linked item record for one bound volume of a serial may be seen in Figure 5.

There can also be one or more order/pay/receipt records (OPRs) linked to each copy statement. An OPR is used to control the ordering, claiming, and receiving of items for a specific copy (including

```
LTNU DONE                                              ACS9292
                                       NOTIS VOLUME HOLDINGS    L4XB
NU SERL LC en 82002028  ISSN 0731-7131 S/STAT c FREQ q S/T p CFR 4/1
Technical services quarterly. Vol. 1, no. 1/2 (fall/winter 1983)-    -- New
   York, N.Y. : Haworth Press, 1983- Haworth Press, 28 E. 22nd St., New York,
   N.Y. 10010
=>001 2D CN $a main $b 020.5 $c T255 $v v. $d 11/29/83
   VH 001 $a 1-2(1983,fall-1985,summer)                       $d 09/26/85
```

FIGURE 4. NOTIS Volume Holdings Record

```
LTNU DONE                                              ACS9292-001-0001
                                       DISPLAY ITEM RECORD    L4XB
NU SERL LC en 82002028  ISSN 0731-7131 S/STAT c FREQ q S/T p CFR 4/1
Technical services quarterly. Vol. 1, no. 1/2 (fall/winter 1983)-    -- New
   York, N.Y. : Haworth Press, 1983- Haworth Press, 28 E. 22nd St., New York,
   N.Y. 10010
=>001  STATUS: 2D LOCN: MAIN                        COPY:
CALL: $b 020.5 $c T255 $v v.                        ITEMS: 1
 LINKED ITEM RECORD
ENUM/CHRON:   v.1-2
MIDSPINE:     1983:Fall-1985:Summer
DEPT LOCATN:
TEMP LOCATN:
ITEM ID:      3 5556 010 750 750
LOAN CODE:    none (no loan)              PIECES:     1
REVIEW:       _ CIRCULATION  _ CATALOG    ACTION:     none
STATUS: A (active)    OVERDUE NOTICES:  0    CREATED:    09/26/85
CHARGES: 1            AVAIL NOTICES:    0    UPDATED:    11/11/85
BROWSES: 0           RECALLS & HOLDS:   0    LAST USE:   11/11/85
NOTE:

DISCHARGED:  11/11/85 12:53 PM  AT  Northwestern Univ Main Library   L9PF
```

FIGURE 5. NOTIS Linked Item Record

178 THE USMARC FORMAT FOR HOLDINGS AND LOCATIONS

check-in of current issues for serials) as well as the handling of all relevant financial transactions. Figure 6 shows an OPR for an active serial subscription.

In the examples of the various kinds of linked records described above, some of the NOTIS design principles are clearly illustrated. At the top of each screen we display selected bibliographic data elements that are actually stored only in the linked bibliographic record. This data display facilitates the use of the various linked records by library staff. The volume holdings record and the item record each carry additional data at the top of the display screen that comes from the copy statement to which they are linked, again to facilitate use of the records by staff.

It is in the online public catalog display of a NOTIS record, however, that the principles of system integration and data nonredundancy are most apparent. LUIS (Library User Information Service) is the online public access component of NOTIS. The LUIS display for a title in the NOTIS database contains data extracted from all the parts of the linked record structure that is used by library staff in their daily work. Full bibliographic data is obtained from the bibliographic record; processing status, location, and call number data

```
LTNU DONE                                                  ACS9292
                                          NOTIS ACQUISITIONS       L4XB
   NU SERL LC sn 82002028   ISSN 0731-7131 S/STAT c FREQ q S/T p CFR 4/1
Technical services quarterly. Vol. 1, no. 1/2 (fall/winter 1983)-      -- New
   York, N.Y. : Haworth Press, 1983- Haworth Press, 28 E. 22nd St., New York,
   N.Y. 10010
PO 001ACS9292   11/29/83
VEND faxon         SHIP 2 INV 2 RUSH 0 MEMO C
   VA The Haworth Press, Inc.;Attn: Circulation Department;75 Griswold Street;
      Binghamton, NY  13904
   NV nv=Faxon title no. 159051
   NO
DIV 001 CCN 001 RTE ci to pr/sdi CLM 200
=> 001 A Vol. 1 (1983)-                               MD 11/29/83 AD none
                          AMT   48.00  FUND 6522-056 CURR      AIN #
=> 004 P 9/86-8/87:inv=021412-157-9:8/1/85           MD 09/19/85 AD none
                          AMT   62.00  FUND 6522-056 CURR      AIN # z
=> 005 P 9/85-8/86(ad chg):inv=790738-4-1:9/20/85    MD 10/09/85 AD none
                          AMT   12.00  FUND 6522-056 CURR      AIN # z
=> 006 P 9/86-8/87(ad chg):inv=951875-3-2:8/15/86    MD 09/08/86 AD none
                          ,       AMT    5.00  FUND 6522-056 CURR      AIN # z
=> 007 P 9/87-8/88:inv=173109-161-11:8/1/86          MD 10/20/86 AD none
                          AMT   62.00  FUND 6522-056 CURR      AIN # z
=> 008 R 3,no.1/2-3/4(1985,fall/winter-1986/sprng/sumr) MD 09/08/86 AD 03/27/87
```

FIGURE 6. NOTIS Order/Pay/Receipt (OPR) Record for a Serial

from the copy holdings record; volume holdings data from the volume holdings record; and circulation status data from the item record(s). For periodicals, up-to-the-minute information on currently received loose issues is obtained from the order/pay/receipt record. In response to a user's request, the LUIS programs retrieve the needed data from the various records and display it in a format designed to facilitate user interpretation. Figure 7 shows the LUIS display for a serial.

NOTIS: THE MFHL PROJECT

The goal of the NOTIS MFHL (MARC Format for Holdings and Locations) implementation project was two-fold: 1) to integrate the data elements needed for control and use of holdings information into the architecture described above; and 2) at the same time, to preserve the basic NOTIS design principles in enhancing the system to provide for maximum utilization of Format data.

A thorough reading and analysis of the Holdings Format indicated that integration of the new data elements into NOTIS would

```
LUIS SEARCH REQUEST:  T=TECHNICAL SERVICES Q
BIBLIOGRAPHIC RECORD -- NO. 2 OF 2 ENTRIES FOUND

Technical services quarterly. -- Vol. 1, no. 1/2 (fall/winter 1983)-      -- New
   York, N.Y. : Haworth Press, 1983-
   v. ; 22 cm.
   Quarterly.
   SUBJECT HEADINGS (Library of Congress; use s= ):
       Library science--Periodicals.
       Library science--Technological innovations--Periodicals.
       Libraries--Automation--Periodicals.

LOCATION: MAIN
CALL NUMBER:  020.5 T255
Current issues in Periodicals
LIBRARY HAS:
   1-2(1983,fall-1985,summer)
   CURRENT ISSUES/VOLUMES:
      3,no.1/2-3/4(1985,fall/winter-1986/sprng/sumr)


TYPE i TO RETURN TO INDEX.  TYPE e TO START OVER.  TYPE h FOR HELP.
TYPE COMMAND AND PRESS ENTER
```

FIGURE 7. LUIS Display for a Serial

be a fairly straightforward task given the existing system design and our previous experience in working with the MARC Formats for bibliographic and authority data. It was also clear from the start that considerably more effort would be required to develop system capabilities for fully utilizing the Holdings Format data, but that we had much to gain from this effort. In defining the scope of the implementation project, we also looked beyond our immediate needs to several other related system enhancements which could logically be built on the foundation we would lay with the MFHL Project. Thus, in developing the project plan for our implementation of the new format, we determined that it would be accomplished in two phases, with each phase to consist of several component subprojects, and we also laid out preliminary plans for further enhancements to the system after completion of the Project.

The overall goal of Phase I, as defined in the plan, included the addition of a new type of Holdings Format-based record to the NOTIS architecture along with the capability to have the system validate some of the data elements in this record. The new record is called the MARC Holdings Record, a name that was soon abbreviated to the acronym "MHLD."

Phase II includes several components, among them the following: enhanced system security to provide detailed control over the terminal operator's ability to create, display, update, and delete MARC Holdings Records; enhanced capabilities for validating data elements in the MARC Holdings Record, including cross-validation of data among several of the variable length fields; an online catalog display version of the holdings data stored in the MARC Holdings Records; several conversion programs to permit loading of machine-readable data from other systems into NOTIS MARC Holdings Records; a simplified nonpublic version of the MARC Holdings Record for use by library staff who, for whatever reasons, find the raw Holdings Format data too complex; and the ability to generate, on request, various forms of output from MARC Holdings Records (e.g., the ability to report serials holdings to a union list on tape).

Postproject plans include providing ongoing support for the Holdings Format with timely implementation of all published updates to the Format and the development of several new projects based on data elements either currently found in the Holdings Format or to be locally defined later by NOTIS in the Holdings Record.

PHASE I: THE MARC HOLDINGS RECORD

In planning for Phase I, there were three major design issues to consider:

- Where and how would the new record fit into the existing architecture?
- What data elements from the Holdings Format would be incorporated into the new NOTIS record?
- What would the record look like to library staff?

Finding a niche in NOTIS for the MARC Holdings Record was an easy task. It was clear from the start that the MARC Holdings Record would eventually replace the NOTIS volume holdings record. The raison d'être for both records is the same — to provide a place in the system to store detailed or summarized holdings data from which the data can be retrieved whenever needed for display to the public through the online catalog and for other purposes. The important difference between them is that the new MARC Holdings Record has full content designation while the old volume holdings record has none. The power and usefulness of the new record far outstrips that of the old and represents a major step forward for NOTIS.

Although the MARC Holdings Record is currently available for use in NOTIS, the old volume holdings record will remain in the record structure until the completion of all the component projects in Phase II. At that time the volume holdings record will be retired.

The second design issue, namely, deciding which of the Holdings Format data elements to incorporate into the new MARC Holdings Record and how, was really a two-part issue requiring separate consideration of the fixed length fields and the variable length fields.

In the former category, the areas of concern were the Leader, Field 007, and Field 008.

The Leader plays an important technical role in the MARC rec-

182 THE USMARC FORMAT FOR HOLDINGS AND LOCATIONS

ord, providing parameters used by the system for processing the record. Much of the information in the Leader, however, is not meaningful to the library employee using the staff mode display version of the record and cannot be supplied or modified by the terminal operator. For this reason the Holdings Format Leader, as such, does not appear on the screen in a NOTIS MARC Holdings Record although it can be constructed when needed for records to be output from NOTIS to other systems.

In NOTIS, we defined a new field in the MARC Holdings Record, Field 000, that includes three data elements from the Format Leader (character positions 05, 06, and 17) that are very important to library staff. Field 000 also contains two data elements from the 008 field of the Format (character positions 00-05 and 26-31). In other words, Field 000 contains the following information:

- Record status (Leader/05) (system-supplied, except in the case of "d" (delete))
- Type of record (Leader/06)
- Encoding level (Leader/17)
- Date record entered in the NOTIS file (008/00-05) (system-supplied)
- Date of latest update to record (008/26-31) (system-supplied)

We grouped these elements together in Field 000 so they would display ahead of all other data elements on the Holdings Record screen, reasoning that, regardless of the level of specificity desired, these elements must be included in the record.

Field 007 had already been incorporated into the NOTIS bibliographic record as defined in the *MARC Formats for Bibliographic Data*. Because we knew that some NOTIS users would want to be able to link MARC Holdings Records for items in different formats to one bibliographic record, we decided to incorporate Field 007 into the Holdings Record as well. Our thinking was that a Holdings Record would not contain an 007 field unless the format of the material represented varied from the format of the material described in the linked bibliographic record. Therefore, we decided that data entry areas for the Field 007 elements would not appear on the MARC Holdings Record screen unless specifically requested by a terminal operator.

In the NOTIS MARC Holdings Record, Field 008 differs somewhat from the MARC Format 008 field. As mentioned above, two data elements from the 008 field (character positions 00-05 and 26-31) of the Format were moved to the Holdings Record 000 field. Two additional data elements were dropped altogether because they are not relevant within the context of NOTIS. These are character positions 17-19 (number of copies reported) and 25 (the composite/copy specific indicator). Because each Holdings Record is linked to a specific copy statement in the NOTIS copy holdings record, it is not possible to have a holdings record that represents more than one copy. The remaining elements in Field 008 were retained intact in our new record. As is the case with the Leader, a standard 008 field in the Format can be constructed when needed in records to be output from NOTIS for transmission to other systems.

Data entry areas for Fields 000, 007, and 008 in the NOTIS MARC Holdings Record were designed to facilitate ease of input and ease of interpretation by the system user. Figure 8 shows how this part of the record looks to the library terminal operator. The individual elements in each of the fields are labelled with brief mnemonic tags. The number of characters that can be typed in each element is controlled by the system as are the specific values that can be entered.

The major issue in our consideration of the variable length fields involved the 852 tag. We had two concerns about this field: 1) the first indicator and a significant number of the subfields have been

```
LTNU DONE                                                    AAA0000-002
                                                   NOTIS MARC HOLDINGS    L8XA
XX SERL LCN     59007716   ISSN 0025-4878 S/STAT c FREQ q S/T p
The Massachusetts review.   Vol. 1 (1959)-   -- Amherst, Mass.
=>002  STATUS: 2T  LOCN: MAIN microform room                COPY:  2
CALL: $b Film 232                                           ITEMS: 11

HOLDINGS RECORD

DT mm/dd/yy R/DT mm/dd/yy STAT n R/T ? E/LEV ?
GMD h SMD d O/R ?  POLAR ?  DIM f REDUC ?  ???  COLOR b EMUL ?  GENER ?  BASE ?
R/STAT ?  MTHD ?  DT/CAN ????  G/RTN ? S/RTN ???  CMPLT ?
LEND ? REPOL ? LAN ???
```

FIGURE 8. Data Entrys Areas for Fields 000,007, and 008

184 THE USMARC FORMAT FOR HOLDINGS AND LOCATIONS

defined to include data that already has a home elsewhere in the NOTIS record structure; and 2) the field as it is laid out in Holdings Format is somewhat of a catch-all designed to hold various miscellaneous kinds of data, many of which do not logically belong in a field labelled "Location/Call Number."

The values for indicator 1 specify the type of classification or shelving scheme used to control the physical items represented by the record. In NOTIS, this type of information is recorded in the Class Code, a one-character subfield that appears in each copy statement in the copy holdings record. Existing NOTIS Class Code values equate to most of the Indicator 1 codes. By defining three new values for this subfield, we were able to provide for all the types of classification and shelving schemes covered in Indicator 1.

Eight of the subfields in Field 852 were already accommodated elsewhere in NOTIS. They include:

$a Institution/location
$b Sublocation/collection
$c Shelving location
$h Classification number
$i Item number
$j Shelving control number
$k Call number prefix/suffix
$p Physical item/piece identification.

All of these data elements except the last one, subfield $p, are included in the NOTIS copy holdings record, specifically in the individual copy statements to which each Holdings Record is linked. The subfield $p data (physical item identification) is stored in the individual item record(s), which are also linked to each copy statement.

Of the other 852 subfields, one is irrelevant in the context of NOTIS, subfield $t (copy number), because it is not possible to have a holdings record that represents more than one copy. The remaining subfields include various kinds of data that need not be kept together in the same field in order to be meaningful.

We ultimately decided that although we would accommodate all the 852 data elements somewhere in the NOTIS record structure,

Peggy Steele 185

Field 852, as such, would not appear in the Holdings Record. With this decision we retained adherence to our basic design principle of no data redundancy in the record structure. We also provided ourselves the opportunity to develop a Holdings Record screen display that would handle the 852 data in a user-friendly way. Further, we in no way hindered our ability to develop conversion programs to be used in importing MARC Holdings Format records from other systems and exporting complete location and holdings data from NOTIS records in the pure Holdings Format.

To accommodate the remaining 852 subfields we defined a series of seven new variable length fields, each of which was given an alphabetic field tag that is at least somewhat mnemonic. Corresponding numeric tags were not defined for these fields. They will carry only the mnemonic tags which will help library staff distinguish them visually from the variable length fields defined in the Format. The alpha-tagged fields, we decided, would appear on the Holdings Record screen below all the other variable length fields, i.e., after the 868 field. This group of fields includes the following:

- *Shelving Data Field (Tag: SHL)*
  In this field, Indicator 1 is undefined and Indicator 2 (Number/ location relationship) equates with Indicator 2 from the 852 field of the Format. There are four subfields. Three of them equate to subfields $f (Location qualifier, coded), $g (Location qualifier noncoded), and $1 (shelving form of title) in Field 852. We defined the fourth subfield to hold a NOTIS location code to be used in conjunction with the coded and noncoded location qualifiers.
- *Individual Collector Data Field (Tag: ICO)*
  In this field, both indicators are undefined. There are two subfields that equate to subfield $d (Name of individual collector) and subfield $e (Address of collector) in Field 852.
- *Physical Condition Data Field (Tag: PHY)*
  In this field, both indicators are undefined. There is one subfield that equates to subfield $q (Physical condition data) in Field 852.
- *Preservation Status Data (Tag: PRS)*
  In this field, both indicators are undefined. There is one sub-

186 THE USMARC FORMAT FOR HOLDINGS AND LOCATIONS

field that equates to subfield $r (Preservation status data) in Field 852.

NOTE: As of this writing, there is a proposal before MARBI to make a number of additions and changes to the Holdings Format to provide additional data elements for preservation information. One of the most important of the proposed changes is the definition of a new Preservation Information field (tag: 846). This proposal is to be considered by MARBI at the 1987 ALA Midwinter meeting. If it is approved as is or in a revised version, NOTIS will incorporate Field 846 and any other accompanying changes into the Holdings Record. Most likely these data elements will appear in the Holdings Record almost exactly as they do in the MARC Holdings Format. The inclusion of these data elements in the record will eliminate the need for our locally defined Preservation Status Data field.

- *Copyright Article Code (Tag: CAC)*
In this field, both indicators are undefined. There is one subfield that equates to subfield $s (Copyright article code) in Field 852.
- *Nonpublic Note (Tag: NNP)*
In this field, both indicators are undefined. There is one subfield that equates to subfield $x (Note, Nonpublic) as defined by MARBI for Field 852 in July 1986.
- *Public Note (Tag: NPU)*
In this field, both indicators are undefined. There is one subfield that equates to subfield $z (Note, Public) as redefined by MARBI in July 1986.

With Field 852 as the only significant exception, we decided that the variable fields would appear in the Holdings Record almost exactly as they do in the Format.

Having found the right place in the NOTIS architecture for our new record and having defined its contents, we moved on to the design of the record display screen for library staff. Because the Holdings Record screen had to be consistent in overall layout with other NOTIS screens and because the Format itself gave us a ready-made structure within which to work, this proved to be a fairly straightforward task. The results can be seen in Figure 9, which shows the holdings data for a printed serial, and Figure 10, which represents the microform version of the same publication.

The heading at the top of each screen contains selected data elements from the bibliographic record and the copy holdings record to which the Holdings Record is linked. The label "HOLDINGS RECORD" follows this display and signals the beginning of the

```
LTNU DONE                                        AAA0000-001
                                         NOTIS MARC HOLDINGS   L8XA
 XX SERL LCN    59007716  ISSN 0025-4878 S/STAT c FREQ q S/T p
The Massachusetts review.  Vol. 1 (1959)-   -- Amherst, Mass.
 =>001 STATUS: 2D LOCN: MAIN                          COPY:
CALL: 9b 805 9c M414                                  ITEMS: 25

 HOLDINGS RECORD

DT 03/12/87 R/DT 05/02/87 STAT c R/T y  E/LEV 4
R/STAT 4  MTHD p  DT/CAN        G/RTN 8  S/RTN ???  CMPLT 1
LEND b  REPOL a  LAN eng

853:30: 96 1 9a v. 9b no. 9u 4 9v r 9i yr. 9j month 9v q 9x 01
863/1:42: 96 1.1 9a 1-21 9i 1959-1980 9v n
863/2:42: 96 1.2 9a 23 9i 1982 9q water damage
863/3:42: 96 1.3 9a 24-26 9i 1983-1985
SHL:   : 9b main,pr 9g current issues
```

FIGURE 9. NOTIS/MARC Holdings Record for a Printed Serial

```
LTNU DONE                                        AAA0000-002
                                         NOTIS MARC HOLDINGS   L8XA
 XX SERL LCN    59007716  ISSN 0025-4878 S/STAT c FREQ q S/T p
The Massachusetts review.  Vol. 1 (1959)-   -- Amherst, Mass.
 =>002 STATUS: 2T LOCN: MAIN microform room       COPY:  2
CALL.: 9b Film 232                                ITEMS: 11

 HOLDINGS RECORD

DT 03/12/87 R/DT 05/12/87 STAT c R/T y E/LEV 4
GMD h SMD d O/R ?  POLAR ?  DIM f REDUC ?  ???  COLOR b EMUL ?  GENER ?  BASE ?
R/STAT 4  MTHD p  DT/CAN        G/RTN 8 S/RTN ???  CMPLT 1
LEND b  REPOL a  LAN eng

843/1:   : 9a Microfilm. 9b Ann Arbor, 9c University Microfilms, 9d 1962-1967
9e 5 reels. 35 mm. 93 v.1-10
843/2:   : 9a Microfilm. 9b Boston, 9c Pilgrim Productions, 9d 1968-1984
9e 5 reels. 35 mm. 93 v.11-22
843/3:   : 9a Microfilm. 9b Boston, 9c Pilgrim Productions, 9d 1984- 9e 1
reel. 35 mm. 93 y.24-26
853:30: 96 1 9a v. 9b no. 9u 4 9v r 9i yr. 9j month 9v q 9x 01
863/1:40: 96 1.1 9a 1-22 9i 1959-1981 9v n
863/2:40: 96 1.2 9a 24-26 9i 1983-1985
```

FIGURE 10. NOTIS/MARC Holdings Record for a Serial Microform

188 *THE USMARC FORMAT FOR HOLDINGS AND LOCATIONS*

MARC holdings record itself. Data entry areas for Fields 000, 007 (if needed), and 008 are grouped together under this label. The variable length fields display below the fixed field area.

PHASE II: OTHER FEATURES

With the completion of our planning for Phase I, we have moved on to dealing with the many complex issues to be resolved in Phase II. Deciding on the public display format for the data in the Holdings Records is among the most important of these issues for two reasons. First, providing accurate, timely, and easy-to-interpret information about the library's holdings to the end user through the online catalog is the ultimate goal of NOTIS. Second, NOTIS users are accustomed to finding complete bibliographic, location, holdings, and circulation status data in the online catalog and will expect that our implementation of the Holdings Format will, if anything, give them even better data than before.

Given NOTIS's general policy of adhering to national standards, we feel that we must give very serious consideration to use of the NISO standards for serial holdings statements (Z39.44) and for nonserial items (Z39.57) in displaying NOTIS holdings data to the public. As of this writing, however, the unsettled state of the two standards precludes rapid decision making. The nonserial standard is still going through the review process. There is also some concern that even though the serials standard has been published, it might be subject to revision to make it more compatible with the nonserial standard.

To complicate the issue further, we have heard some sentiment on the part of our users that it might be preferable to design our own public display conventions. In other words, not everyone finds the NISO display conventions totally satisfactory for communicating information about the library's holdings to the user community. At NOTIS the needs expressed by our users are of paramount concern to systems development staff. Obviously, in this case, we need to balance expressed user needs carefully against our policy of adherence to national standards. Possibly we will opt to implement two display formats, a NISO-based format and a NOTIS-designed format, and allow each NOTIS installation to choose the one most satisfactory for its users.

Another factor to be considered in deciding on the public display format is the likelihood that many Holdings Records will contain holdings data in both the highly formatted 863/4/5 fields and the free-text 866/7/8 fields. Data from the 863/4/5 fields can be machine-manipulated with relative ease into whatever display format(s) we decide on. Data from the 866/7/8 fields, on the other hand, has to be used as is. If we are to display data from both sets of fields in the online catalog, the result may possibly be confusing to library patrons. Deciding on exactly what data from these fields to show in our online catalog and how to mesh data stored in two different formats into a meaningful and consistent display will be no easy task. Quite possibly there is no completely satisfactory solution.

A second project of major significance in Phase II is the development of editing routines to cross-validate the information supplied by library staff in the 853/863, 854/864, and 855/865 pairs among the variable length fields. The correctness and consistency of the data in these field pairs is crucial for full utilization of the compression and expansion capabilities provided for in the Format. If the content of the various enumeration subfields in an 863 field, for example, does not correspond appropriately to the terms designated in the enumeration subfields of the linked 853 field, the data is meaningless for purposes of public display, report-generation, or any other use that might be made of it. Correct data in the field pairs is also essential for some of the Holdings Record-based development projects to be undertaken by NOTIS after the completion of Phase II.

A third Phase II project is the design of a simplified staff display version of the Holdings Record that will enable staff at all levels to view and easily interpret all data pertinent to the library's holdings. The assumption underlying the inclusion of this particular project in Phase II is that not all staff will want to become familiar enough with the Holdings Format content designation features to be able to read and correctly interpret a straight MARC Holdings Record with ease, but that all staff should nonetheless have ready access to all the data stored there. We want to be able to provide a display of data in clearly labelled, easily readable fields that any member of the staff can feel comfortable consulting.

Another important project in Phase II is the development of two types of conversion programs. One, for existing NOTIS customers, will move any holdings data currently in volume holdings records to the 866/7/8 fields in the new Holdings Records. The other, intended primarily for new customers, will permit machine-readable holdings and location data from other systems to be loaded into NOTIS. A related project will involve the development of output programs to permit communication in print, on tape, or via electronic file transfer of bibliographic, location, and holdings data to other systems, to the utilities, to union list projects, etc.

POST PHASE II

One of the most exciting aspects of the NOTIS MARC Holdings Format implementation project is that the completion of Phase I and Phase II, while a truly significant accomplishment in itself, will also give us a foundation on which to build other new features to facilitate the processing and control of all types of library materials, especially serials. The NOTIS implementation of the Format results in a Holdings Record that gives us control over a great deal of data at the copy level. This information can and will be used by NOTIS, in conjunction with other data elements to be defined in the future, to expand the capabilities of the system in a variety of ways. Examples of such future projects include the development of a NOTIS binding control function and the enhancement of the serials control function to allow for predictive check-in of selected serial titles.

The Display of
Serial Holdings Statements

Marjorie E. Bloss

The relationship between the *American National Standard for Information Sciences – Serial Holdings Statements* (ANSI Z39.44-1986) and the *USMARC Format for Holdings and Locations* is identical to that of *Anglo-American Cataloguing Rules*, 2nd edition (*AACR2*) and the various MARC formats for bibliographic information. The standard on serial holdings statements and *AACR2* define the requirements for identifying, recording, and displaying holdings and bibliographic data. Neither *Serial Holdings Statements* nor *AACR2* in any way addresses the machine storage of those data. On the other hand, the *USMARC Format for Holdings and Locations* and the MARC formats for bibliographic information provide only for the machine storage of the content designation of holdings, location, and bibliographic data. They do not concern themselves at all with the display of holdings or bibliographic data for the end user.

Technological reasons aside, the fact that the MARC formats were developed after decisions were made concerning the record content for both bibliographic and holdings data makes perfect sense. The MARC formats can, in effect, be considered the closet organizers of the library world. The analogy is one of an immense storage closet with numerous compartments of varying sizes (the MARC formats) and the intended contents of those compartments (bibliographic and holdings data). Before sectioning off the storage closet one must have some idea of what it is going to contain. Books, camping equipment, and the old hamster cage you keep

---

Marjorie E. Bloss is Manager, Resource Sharing Department, OCLC, Inc.

192   THE USMARC FORMAT FOR HOLDINGS AND LOCATIONS

"just in case" require very different types and sizes of compartments than do those for clothes and shoes. The creators of the MARC formats must first be intimately aware of the pieces of information they intend to store before they create those formats.

Much has already been said in this volume about the *USMARC Format for Holdings and Locations* with regard to its development, implementation, and use. This paper will discuss holdings statements from the other side of the fence, namely, the display or order of serial holdings data as a user would view those data rather than as a machine would store them. While there have been many, many techniques over the years for displaying serial holdings information, the major concepts of the display of that information as detailed in the newly published *American National Standard for Information Sciences – Serial Holdings Statements* are the focal point of this paper.

No standard should be created without a careful investigation of earlier, related developments. Accordingly, a short historical perspective of the recording and displaying of serial holdings statements prior to 1986 is in order before discussing the concepts of serial holdings as seen in the new standard.

EXAMINING OUR PAST

In general, the recording of holdings statements is considerably more important for serial publications than it is for monographic ones. This is due to the fact that no library has ever been able to own every issue of every serial. Libraries creating or maintaining internal serial lists or participating in union lists of serials need not only to represent the bibliographic information of the titles they own in a uniform manner, but also to indicate which issues, numbers, and volumes of those particular titles are in their collections. For many years, holdings statements as formatted in the multivolume sets issued by the Library of Congress, *A Union List of Serials of the United States and Canada*, and its successor, *New Serial Titles*, were considered as *de facto* standards both in terms of the punctuation used and the order of enumeration and chronology (numbering and years). Even so, many libraries or groups of libraries developed their own methods for the recording of holdings information. User frustration was quite high due to the wide variance in punctuation and symbols found in different lists.

The CONSER Project, begun in 1975, had a major impact not only on the need to standardize serials bibliographic data for the purpose of sharing those data, but also on the need for the uniform representation of serial holdings statements as well. Over the past 10 years, two standards committees of the National Information Standards Organization (NISO) Z39 have worked to develop standards for serial holdings statements. The first of these two committees, Standards Committee (SC) 40, began its work in 1975 on a standard for serial holdings statements at the summary level. At this level, serial holdings statements are recorded at the primary or most inclusive levels of enumeration and chronology. The result of SC 40's labors was published in 1980 as the American National Standard Institute's *Standard for Serial Holdings Statements at the Summary Level.*[1]

Even before the work of SC 40 had been completed, another Standards Committee, SC E, began working on a second standard for serial holdings statements. The goal of this standard was to standardize the display of serial holdings statements at the detailed, or issue-specific level. This standard would, therefore, serve as a complement to the standard for serial holdings statements at the summary level.

Because of the *Standard for Serial Holdings Statements at the Summary Level*, SC E' s draft standard ran into a few roadblocks. Considerable comment from the NISO voting membership and potential users of the draft standard raised some very major concerns. The majority of those concerns centered on the inconsistencies found between the standard for serial holdings statements at the summary level and the draft standard for serial holdings statements at the detailed level.

In order to reconcile the differences between the two standards, NISO Z39 sponsored a meeting in May 1983 with funds from the Council on Library Resources, Inc. In addition to the members of the two NISO Standards Committees who either had developed or were developing the standards for serial holdings statements, were observers from the Library of Congress, the Southeastern ARL Serials Project, NISO Standards Committee W (which is preparing a standard for the holdings of nonserial materials), and the IFLA Section on Serial Publications. Relatively early on in this meeting, members of the two NISO serial holdings committees and the observers unanimously recommended "that a single Z39 standard for serial holdings statements be developed, encompassing both the detailed and summary levels."[2]

As a result of this recommendation, the charge to Standards Committee E was revised to include the defining of serial holdings statements at both the summary and detailed levels. The resulting standard was approved by the NISO voting membership and in 1986, was published by the American National Standards Institute as the *American National Standard for Information Sciences — Serial Holdings Statements* (ANSI Z39.44-1986). Now that this new standard for serial holdings statements has been issued, the earlier ANSI standard, the *American National Standard for Serial Holdings Statements at the Summary Level*, (ANSI Z39.42-1980) will be withdrawn.

Even so, the 1986 standard for serial holdings statements owes a considerable amount to the preceding standard. While there are some major differences between the two, there are also many similarities. The *Standard for Serial Holdings Statements at the Summary Level* contained the concept of different levels of holdings specificity, each one building on the information of the previous level. This same approach is found in the new standard. Many of the data elements and their coding are identical in the two standards. There have been, of course, some additions to the data elements, changes in their order, and changes in the punctuation used.

Standards Committee E was very much aware of the user community that had already created many thousands of holdings statements according to the summary standard, and the uproar that would result if that community were informed that all holdings statements created prior to 1986 were null and void. As a result, several "grandfather" clauses are found in the *Standard for Serial Holdings Statements*, recognizing the existence of holdings statements created according to the summary standard and their validity.

Now that a short overview of the history of the representation of holdings statements has been given, it is time to examine the new ANSI standard on serial holdings statements and its effect on the display of holdings information.

THE SCOPE OF THE STANDARD
FOR SERIAL HOLDINGS STATEMENTS

The "Abstract" found at the beginning of the new holdings standard for serials describes the standard very succinctly. It states:

> This standard establishes rules and punctuation for preparing consistent, standardized records of the bibliographic units of serials located at a particular institution. Such serial holdings statements can be prepared at four levels of specificity: Level 1 identifies the serial and the holding institution; Level 2 adds coded data on such aspects as completeness of holdings and acquisition status; Level 3 adds enumeration and chronology information in a summary form; Level 4 provides enumeration and chronology in a detailed form. The specific data areas, data elements, and punctuation to be used in serial holdings statements are identified, and specifications are provided for displaying the data elements within data areas.[3]

Section 1.2, Scope,[4] further identifies some of the major characteristics of the standard. It states that the standard will deal only with serial holdings, and only with the positive display of those holdings (Sections 1.2.1 and 1.2.2). Section 1.2.5 of the standard states that while the standard does prescribe the sequence of the data element display within an area, it does not prescribe the recording or display sequence of data areas within the holdings statement itself. Thus, users may rearrange the order of the data *area* displays according to their preference. The standard's Section 1.2.6 emphasizes that the guidelines found in this standard are independent of any cataloging system such as *AACR2*, latest or successive entry, the International Serials Data System, or the International Standard for Bibliographic Description. Neither the form of the representa-

196 THE USMARC FORMAT FOR HOLDINGS AND LOCATIONS

tion of the holding library, nor the serial identifier, nor a medium for transferring, storing, or display of data are included in the standard (Sections 1.2.8, 1.2.4, and 1.2.7).

PUNCTUATION USED IN THE STANDARD

Section 3 and Table 1 of the standard define 10 elements of punctuation that are to be used with the representation of serial holdings statements as is necessary. These 10 and their primary purposes include:

1. *Hyphen* — Used when recording enumeration and chronology data for the purposes of showing either inclusive or ongoing holdings, e.g., v. 1(1970)-v. 3(1972) or v. 1(1970)-   .
2. *Comma* — Used in enumeration or chronology data to reflect a break or gap in a range of holdings. Also used to separate data elements in the location data area and the status data area, e.g., v. 1(1970), v. 5(1974) and (a,ta,0,4,8).
3. *Diagonal* — Used as a connector when either enumeration or chronology covers more than a single volume or period of coverage, e.g., v. 1/2(1966) or 1967/1968.
4. *Question mark* — Represents an unknown quantity in a date, e.g., 194?
5. *Colon* — Serves as a delimiter between two different levels of enumeration : enumeration or chronology : chronology, e.g., v. 1:no. 1(1983:Jan.).
6. *Semicolon* — Indicates a nongap break occurring when an item has not been published, e.g., v. 3(1942);v. 4(1945).
7. *Space* — Separates data elements within a data area.
8. *Parentheses* — Separates enumeration and chronology when these data elements are recorded together. Also encloses the status data area data elements upon display (see item 2).
9. *Equal sign* — Separates alternative numbering schemes in enumeration data, e.g., v. 4:no. 3 = no. 33.
10. *Square brackets* — Encloses a supplied date in chronology data, e.g. [1968].

DISPLAY OF HOLDINGS FOUND IN THE
ANSI SERIAL HOLDINGS STANDARD

As was previously stated, the ANSI standard for serial holdings statements contains four levels of holdings, each at a progressively greater level of specificity. The user of the standard must decide which of the four is most appropriate (Section 1.3.2), or whether different levels are appropriate for different serial publications or functions. This concept is somewhat similar to the three levels of bibliographic description found in *AACR2*, each one consisting of more information than the one before. A library might decide to use *AACR2*'s Level 1 for light-reading paperback books whose shelf life is limited, as opposed to using Level 3 for a rare manuscript. Similarly, holdings reported at a detailed level (Level 4 in the holdings standard) may be very useful for a check-in record where holdings at a summary level (the standard's Level 3) may be more appropriate for union list reporting. The users must decide what is most appropriate for their needs.

LEVEL 1 HOLDINGS STATEMENTS

Level 1 holdings in the *ANSI Standard for Serial Holdings Statements* is the most basic of the four levels of holdings information found in the *Standard*. It consists of two primary pieces of information: the serial identifier and the identification of the library owning the serial, or the Location Data Area as it is termed in the standard. No provisions are made regarding the "proper" representation of either the serial identifier or the institution identifier. Section 1.2.4 of the standard states that "the method of identifying the serial is excluded from this standard. However, this standard requires that the serial holdings statement be linked to an identification of the serial (for example, a bibliographic description, ISSN, or CODEN)."

Section 1.2.8 parallels this rule, but for institutional identifiers. It states that "specifications of the type or scheme of institution code or sublocation identifier is excluded from this standard." Thus, an

198   THE USMARC FORMAT FOR HOLDINGS AND LOCATIONS

institution's fully spelled out name may be used, as may a code such as an NUC symbol, a numeric representation, or a code assigned by a bibliographic network (Figure 1).

LEVEL 2 HOLDINGS STATEMENTS

The recording of serial holdings at the second level incorporates the information found in Level 1 plus three additional data areas: the Date of Report Data Area; the Status Data Area, and; the Local Notes Data Area (Figure 2). The date of report is a mandatory data area when reporting holdings at Levels 2, 3, and 4, requiring eight digits when representing that date.

The Status Data Area consists of five coded elements: the Type of Holdings Designator; the Physical Form Designator; the Completeness Designator; the Acquisitions Status Designator, and the Retention Designator. Representation of all five coded elements is mandatory for Levels 2, 3, and 4 of the standard.

The Type of Holdings Designator indicates if the displayed holdings are reported at the summary or detailed level, or if they are subordinately described supplements or indexes. (A more detailed explanation of these concepts will be given later in this paper.) In the case of Level 2 reporting where enumeration and chronology

```
                              Serial
                            Identifier

Journal of feline psychology. -- Vol. 1, no. 1 (Jan. 1980)-
        Mousetrap, Ill. : Purrfection Press, 1980-
            v. ; quarterly.
        Separately numbered supplements accompany some issues.
        Indexes issued every two years.



Library A


Location Data
Area
```

FIGURE 1. Level 1 Holdings Statement

Marjorie E. Bloss

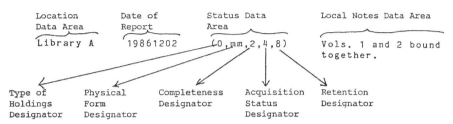

FIGURE 2. Level 2 Holdings Statement

data are not specifically displayed, the code "0" is used, indicating that no bibliographic units are recorded in the holdings statement.

The Physical Form Designator reflects the physical form of the bibliographic units recorded in the holdings statement. Appendix C in the standard is used in conjunction with this data element. This Appendix consists of 15 two-letter alphabetic codes. Among the ones more commonly used are: Microfilm cartridge (hb); Microfilm cassette (hc); Microfilm reel (hd); Microfiche (he); Multiple media (mm); Text (ta); Large print (tb); Braille (tc), and; Unspecified (zu). Rather than burden the user with the need to remember these codes or refer to a table listing them, the instructions found at the beginning of Appendix C state: "In recording the physical form designation, either the codes OR the equivalent display text may be used."

The next three codes in the Status Data Area are identical in scope to those in the *ANSI Standard for Serial Holdings Statements at the Summary Level*. The first of these is the Completeness Designator, which reflects how much of the published run of a serial is held by the reporting institution. In order to determine the appropriate numeric designation, the reporting institution must estimate its

200 THE USMARC FORMAT FOR HOLDINGS AND LOCATIONS

holdings on a percentage basis at the time of reporting. Reassuringly, the standard tells us that this does not necessarily require that an inventory must be taken. Four coded values comprise this element. A "0" indicates that the information is not available, not applicable, or that the retention is limited. The coded value "1" indicates that an institution holds between 95%-100% of a published run of a title. A "2" represents 50%-94% of a published run, and a "3" represents scattered holdings, or less than 50%.

The Acquisition Status Designator informs the user if the reporting institution is or is not currently receiving the title. Again, a code of "0" indicates that information is not available. A "4" represents a title that is currently received. A "5" indicates a title that is not currently received. It should be stressed that the reporting institution must base this code on current receipt rather than whether or not the title is currently being published.

The Retention Designator (known as the Nonretention Code in the *Summary Holdings Standard*) indicates, as the name implies, whether or not the reporting institution retains the title. Four coded values have been designated. Again, a "0" indicates that information is not available. An "8" reflects that all units are permanently retained. A "6" represents limited retention, and a "7" indicates that units are not kept at all.

A final data area that is optional for use with a Level 2, 3, or 4 holdings statement is the Local Notes Data Area. Section 4.7 of the standard explains the conditions under which Local Notes may be included in a holdings statement. It states: "Local notes are strictly for information of a local nature that cannot be provided in other data elements yet which may be of assistance in interpreting the holdings statement. . . . " The Local Notes Data Area can include such information as a library's retention policy, local access restrictions, physical conditions of volumes held in the library, and for Levels 2 and 3 only, information concerning the physical medium (microfilm, text, microfiche, etc.) of the volumes held. The standard is emphatic on what sort of information should *not* be included in Local Notes Data Area. Information of a bibliographic nature, such as numbering irregularities, shall not be included in the Local Notes Data Area.

LEVEL 3 HOLDINGS STATEMENTS

Level 3 holdings statements describe serial holdings at the summary level, that is, holdings at the most inclusive levels of enumeration and chronology data. The data elements of enumeration and chronology are mandatory in Level 3 and are added to the information reported in Levels 1 and 2. In order to accommodate the users of the earlier serial holdings standard, the reporting of enumeration and chronology can follow one of two patterns of display in the current standard.

The Summary Holdings Standard specified that strings of enumeration data were to be followed by strings of corresponding chronology data.[5] The new standard, *Serial Holdings Statements*, includes two options for the display of these data *at the summary level only*. Section 7.2.2 of the standard, "Order of Recorded and Display Data," describes these two options. Option A requires the display of holdings as enumeration data followed immediately by its corresponding chronology data (Figure 3). Option B, on the other hand, adheres to the pattern first described in the Summary Holdings Standard: that strings of enumeration data should be followed by strings of their corresponding chronology data (Figure 4). Regardless of which option is used, the Type of Holdings Designator will be given a code of "a," thus indicating that the holdings are reported at the summary level.

Users of *Serial Holdings Statements* will have to decide which of the two options for reporting serial holdings at the summary level is more appropriate for their needs. If they had previously used the *ANSI Standard for Serial Holdings Statements at the Summary Level*, they might be tempted to continue to use Option B (enumeration and chronology data recorded separately) for consistency of format. One factor to weigh, however, is whether the reporting library plans to report holdings at the detailed level (Level 4). Enumeration and chronology data *must* be displayed together at this level. There is no option. If Option B were used for summary holdings statements, a mix of formats would result if Level 4 were used. One way to remedy this situation might be to convert already-created holdings statements to Option A gradually, whenever they needed modification. Ultimately, the decision of which option to

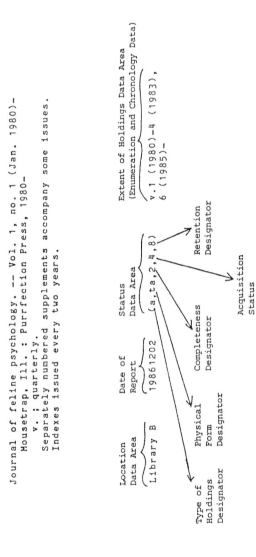

FIGURE 3. Level 3, Summary, Holdings Statement: Option A

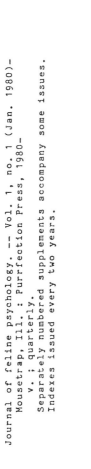
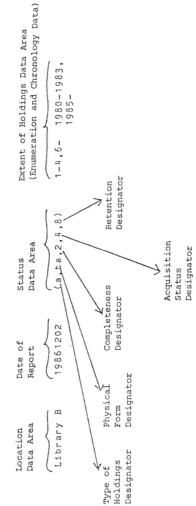

FIGURE 4. Level 3, Summary, Holdings Statement: Option B

204 *THE USMARC FORMAT FOR HOLDINGS AND LOCATIONS*

follow and whether to reformat holdings data must be made at the local level.

THE USE OF CAPTIONS WITH ENUMERATION AND CHRONOLOGY DATA

The "Glossary of Terms and Bibliographic Elements" in both the summary holdings standard and the new one define a caption as: "An alphabetic word or phrase attached as a prefix to the enumeration data that describes the type of data (for example, volume, Band, Heft, part, number or tome)." The *Summary Holdings Standard* was adamant on its stand on captions. Under no circumstances were captions to be used with enumeration data.[6]

When it drafted the new standard, Standards Committee E recommended that captions should be required in a serial holdings statement if they appeared on the publication. Because this was in direct contradiction to the instructions in the earlier standard, a compromise was in order. In the same way that Standards Committee E made allowances for the users of the *Summary Holdings Standard* by including two possibilities for recording enumeration and chronology, they included a "grandfather" clause for users of the *Serials Summary Holdings Standard* regarding captions.

This "grandfather" clause is closely linked to the options for displaying enumeration and chronology data. If Option A is used for a summary holdings statement (enumeration and chronology data are reported together), captions are required if they appear on the publication. If Option B is used (strings of enumeration are followed by their corresponding strings of chronology), captions are required only if they are immediately available. As with the order of display for enumeration and chronology data, only users reporting Level 3 (summary) holdings may optionally omit or include captions.

LEVEL 4 HOLDINGS STATEMENTS

Perhaps the biggest difference between the *ANSI Standard for Serial Holdings Statements at the Summary Level* and the new standard for serial holdings statements is that the latter includes specific rules for formatting and displaying serial holdings at the detailed or issue-specific level. A holdings statement at this level includes the library identifier of Level 1, the coded information of Level 2, and issue-specific enumeration and chronology data. The Type of Holdings Designator is coded "b," thus indicating that the enumeration and chronology data following will be at the issue-specific level.

Unlike serial holdings displayed at the summary level (Level 3), the user is given *no* option for the order of recording enumeration and chronology data for Level 4 holdings. Enumeration must be followed immediately by its corresponding chronology as in Option A of a summary holdings statement. A Level 4 holdings statement is also displayed differently from a summary holdings statement in that a statement at this level does not permit for an open-ended holdings statement (that is, ending with a hyphen), since all holdings must be presented (Section 8.3.4). A hyphen, therefore, must never be the last element when recording holdings at the detailed level (Figure 5).

HOLDINGS STATEMENTS FOR SUPPLEMENTS AND INDEXES

Sections 8.5 and 8.6 of the serial holdings standard concern themselves with the reporting of holdings statements for supplements and indexes. Supplements and indexes that are serials in their own right and are cataloged separately from the parent title will have their holdings statements attached to the appropriate bibliographic descriptions. Supplements and indexes that are identified only in the Notes Area of the bibliographic description, however, are considered to exist below the summary level. Therefore, when creating holdings statements for them, the principles for a Level 4 (detailed) holdings statement apply.

A separate holdings statement for a subordinately described supplement or index will be required in addition to a holdings statement for the parent title. If, for example, a parent title had both supplements and indexes described in notes, three separate holdings statements must be created for each one, assuming, of course, that the reporting library held some or all of all three.

The Type of Holdings Designator must be coded appropriately

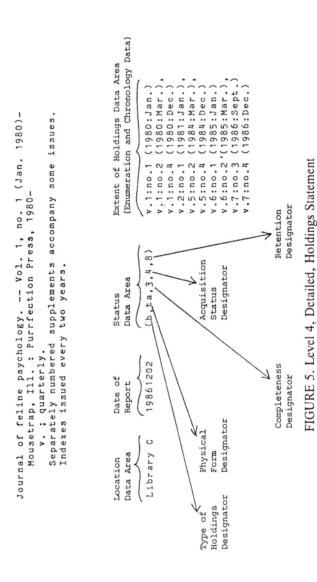

FIGURE 5. Level 4, Detailed, Holdings Statement

for each statement. In the case of the parent title, the code would appear as either an "a" or a "b," contingent upon whether the holdings statement was reported at the summary or detailed level. The Type of Holdings Designator for the subordinately described supplement would be coded as "c" (supplement); the code for the subordinately described index as "d" (index). The enumeration and chronology data for each would be recorded in the appropriate holdings statement (Figure 6).

LEVEL 4 COMPRESSED HOLDINGS STATEMENTS

Section 8.3 of the *Serial Holdings Standard* describes the concept of compressed holdings statements for holdings at the detailed level. A Level 4 holdings statement may be compressed if no gap exists at the lowest hierarchical level. The data may continue to be compressed so long as no gaps exist within the reported levels of enumeration and/or chronology data. As a result, a detailed level, compressed holdings statement can very quickly begin to resemble a summary holdings statement (Figures 7 and 8).

According to Section 1.3.2 of the standard, however, a Level 3 holdings statement "can at best be indicative and not authoritative" with regard to the completeness of the holdings. Section 1.3.2 goes

```
Journal of feline psychology. -- Vo. 1, no. 1 (Jan. 1980)-
       Mousetrap, Ill. : Purrfection Press, 1980-
          v. ; quarterly.
       Separately numbered supplements accompany some issues.
       Indexes issued every two years.



Library D        19861202       (a,ta,1,4,8)      v.1 (1980)-

Library D        19861202       (c,ta,1,4,8)      no.1 (1983) no.2
                                                  (1985) no.3.(1985)
                                                  no.4 (1986)

Library D        19861202       (d,ta,1,4,8)      1980/1981 1982/1983
                                                  1984/1985
```

FIGURE 6. Level 4 Holdings Statement, Subordinately Described Supplements and Indexes

208   THE USMARC FORMAT FOR HOLDINGS AND LOCATIONS

```
Journal of feline psychology. -- Vol. 1, no. 1 (Jan. 1980)-
     Mousetrap, Ill. : Purrfection Press, 1980-
        v. ; quarterly.
     Separately numbered supplements accompany some issues.
     Indexes issued every two years.



Library E        19861202      (b,ta,2,4,8)      v.1:no.1 (1980:Jan.)-
                                                 v.1:no.4 (1980:Dec.),
                                                 v.3:no.1 (1982:Jan.)-
                                                 v.3:no.4 (1982:Dec.)
                                                 v.4:no.1 (1983:Jan.)-
                                                 v.4:no.4 (1983:Dec.)
                                                 v.5:no.1 (1984:Jan.)-
                                                 v.5:no.4 (1984:Dec.),
                                                 v.7:no.1 (1986:Jan.)
                                                 v.7:no.2 (1986:Mar.)
                                                 v.7:no.3 (1986:Sept.)
                                                 v.7:no.4 (1986:Dec.)
```

FIGURE 7. Level 4, Detailed, Compressed Holdings Statement

```
Library E could compress its holdings even further.  Their
display would then be very similar to a Level 3, Summary,
Holdings Statement.


Journal of feline psychology. -- Vol. 1, no. 1 (Jan. 1980)-
     Mousetrap, Ill. : Purrfection Press, 1980-
        v. ; quarterly.
     Separately numbered supplements accompany some issues.
     Indexes issued every two years.



Library E        19861202      (b,ta,2,4,8)      v.1 (1980), v.3
                                                 (1982)-v.5 (1984),
                                                 v.7 (1986)
```

FIGURE 8. Level 4, Detailed, Compressed Holdings Statement

on to say that a "Level 4 [holdings statement] is the authoritative statement that gives the specific, detailed holdings of a serial held by a reporting institution. Therefore, the holdings reported in a Level 4 holdings statement can be assumed to be complete, whether those holdings are reported in issue-specific detail or in compressed form.

GAPS IN HOLDINGS

Any library user who has spent 5 minutes attempting to track down journal articles will very quickly discover the existence of gaps in the library's holdings. The causes of this depressing fact are numerous and no simple remedy will be found in this paper. How the *ANSI Standard on Serial Holdings Statements* represents those gaps in a serial holdings statement, however, will be described.

The new standard for serial holdings statements states, as did the one before it, that holdings shall be reported in a positive manner; in other words, report what is held, not what is lacking (Section 7.2.4). A comma is used to indicate a gap in holdings. The standard's instructions differ for reporting a gap in holdings depending on whether holdings are reported at the Summary Level (Level 3), or at the Detailed Level (Level 4).

In the case of the former, "determination of when a gap occurs shall be based on whether or not any portion of a bibliographic unit is held by the reporting library." Thus a library retaining 1 issue out of 12 that constitute a volume would report those holdings at the volume level if a summary holdings statement were used. Standard Committee E felt this was appropriate for a summary holdings statement. For a detailed holdings statement, however, users are to report each issue held by the institution. Therefore, a gap will be represented by a comma whenever an issue is missing.

SERIAL TITLES IN MULTIPLE PHYSICAL FORMATS

As had been mentioned previously, the *American National Standard for Information Sciences – Serial Holdings Statements* states in Section 1.2.6 that "the guidelines set forth in this standard for generating, recording, and displaying holdings statements are independent of any cataloging system. . . ." As a result, the question of how many bibliographic records a reporting library should use for different physical formats (i.e., one bibliographic record for all physical formats, or one bibliographic record for each physical format) is not really an issue in the standard. What the standard *does* do is attempt to accommodate the reporting library, whatever its decision.

210   THE USMARC FORMAT FOR HOLDINGS AND LOCATIONS

Section 1.3.3 of the standard pertains to the creation of holdings statements for multiple physical formats of the same title. The first option that the standard allows is for the reporting library to use separate bibliographic records for each physical format. Under these circumstances, the relevant holdings information will be found under the bibliographic record for that particular physical format. The Physical Form Designator will be coded or spelled out to reflect those holdings (Figure 9).

The second option permitted by the standard may be used only for the first three levels of the standard. In these cases, one holdings statement combining multiple physical formats may be used with a single bibliographic record for all physical formats of the title. The Physical Form Designator is coded "mm," Multiple Media. Pre-

```
(1) Record for the paper copy:

Journal of feline psychology. -- Vol. 1, no. 1 (Jan. 1980)-
        Mousetrap, Ill. : Purrfection Press, 1980-


Library F      19861202      (a,ta,1,4,8)      v.1 [1980)-
               Other holdings in microfiche and microfilm.


(2) Record for the microfiche copy:

Journal of feline psychology [microform]. -- Vol. 1, no. 1
        (Jan. 1980)-
        Mousetrap, Ill. : Purrfection Press, 1980-


Library F      19861202  (a,he,3,5,8)      v.1 (1980)-v.2 (1981)
               Other holdings in hard copy and microfilm.


(3) Record for the microfilm copy:

Journal of feline psychology [microform]. -- Vol. 1, no. 1
        (Jan. 1980)-
        Mousetrap, Ill. : Purrfection Press, 1980-


Library F      19861202  (a,hd,2,4,8)      v.6 (1985)-
               Other holdings in hard copy and microfiche.
```

FIGURE 9. Separate Bibliographic Records for Each Physical Format of the Title (In each case, the Physical Form Designator will reflect the physical format of the reported holdings. Optionally, the library could use a Local Note to inform users that the library owned holdings in other physical formats.)

sumably, the reporting library has the option of using the Local Notes Area to identify which volumes are held in what physical format. The construction of the note would be determined locally (Figure 10).

The last option allowed by the standard again permits the use of a single bibliographic record for all physical formats of a title. This time, however, a separate holdings statement is created for each physical format and is linked to the serial identifier. While a library reporting a Level 3 (summary) holdings statement using one bibliographic record can choose between this option and the second one described above, a library reporting holdings at the detailed level has no such choice. The reporting library using one bibliographic record for all physical formats of a title and reporting holdings at the detailed level must create separate holdings statements for each physical format under that one bibliographic record. No other option is permitted (Figure 11).

As with the options for deciding the order of enumeration and chronology for Level 3 (summary) holdings, the decision of how to report the holdings of a title in multiple physical formats is a local one. Again, the reporting library (or libraries if a union list of serials is the goal) may wish to base this decision on how that record is going to be used. Union lists of serials participants may feel that one bibliographic record with a single holdings statement combining all physical formats per reporting library is most appropriate for their needs. Users of the standard for serial check-in purposes, however, might feel very differently. In their cases, separate holdings statements for each physical format are absolutely essential. The

```
Journal of feline psychology. -- Vol. 1, no. 1 (Jan. 1980)-
     Housetrap, Ill. : Purrfection Press, 1980-

Library G      19861202       (a,mm,1,4,8)       v.1 (1980)-
               Paper copy = v.1 (1980)-       ; Microfiche =
               v.1(1980)-v.2 (1981); Microfilm = v.6 (1985)-
```

FIGURE 10. A Single Bibliographic Record With One Holdings Statement For All Physical Formats (In this case, the Physical Form Designator is coded "mm" for Multiple Media. A Local Note is used to indicate which volumes are held in what physical format. The Standard does *not* specify the wording, punctuation, format, or display of this local note.)

212 THE USMARC FORMAT FOR HOLDINGS AND LOCATIONS

```
Journal of feline psychology. -- Vol. 1, no. 1 (Jan. 1980)-
     Mousetrap, Ill. : Purrfection Press, 1980-
        v. ; quarterly.
     Separately numbered supplements accompany some issues.
     Indexes issued every two years.


Library F      19861202     (a,ta,1,4,8)     v.1 (1980)-

Library F      19861202     (a,he,3,5,8)     v.1 (1980)-v.2 (1981)

Library F      19861202     (a,hd,3,4,8)     v.6 (1985)-
```

FIGURE 11. A Single Bibliographic Record For All Physical Formats With A Separate Holdings Statement For Each Physical Format

standard identifies these options for its users and permits them the flexibility to select what best suits their needs.

CONCLUSION

This paper has attempted to describe the major components of the new *American National Standard for Information Sciences – Serial Holdings Statements*. Including all the rules described in the standard is impossible, yet some flavor of its general concepts should have become evident from the examples and explanations found in this paper. The standard is very new; so new, in fact, that its application in many cases is based primarily on speculation. Time and experience are needed in order to work through these applications and any necessary interpretations. This sort of process is typical of a new standard, and in no way diminishes the standard's strength.

The "Foreword" to the *USMARC Format for Holdings and Locations* states that "the most critical need [for this format] is for the ability to communicate and exchange holdings and location information in a standard manner."[7] The need for standardization and uniformity is true not only when describing the need for a communications format for the machine storage of holdings information, but for the display of that information as well. The *USMARC Format for Holdings and Locations* and the *American National Standard for Information Sciences – Serial Holdings Statements* will provide the library community with two very powerful tools. The first allows for a standard communications format for holdings statements for all material. The second gives guidance for the uniform display of serial holdings statements specifically. The importance of these two mechanisms working together cannot be underestimated in this day and age when online catalogs and resource sharing are becoming more and more the norm.

NOTES

1. American National Standards Institute, *American National Standard for Serial Holdings Statements at the Summary Level*, Z39.42-1980 (New York: The Institute, 1980).

2. American National Standards Institute, National Information Standards Organization (Z39), *Serial Holdings Statements*, Z39.44-198x, final draft, DL:85-005 (Washington, D.C., NISO Z39, 1985), 4A.

3. American National Standards Committee on Library and Information Sciences and Related Publishing Practices, Z39. Subcommittee E: Serial Holdings Statements, *American National Standard for Information Sciences — Serial Holdings Statements,* Z39.44-1986 (New York: The Institute, 1986), Abstract.

4. All sections cited in this paper will be found in the *American National Standard for Information Sciences — Serial Holdings Statements*, Z39.44-1986.

5. ANSI *Standard for Serial Holdings Statements at the Summary Level*, Section 5.2.2, p. 16.

6. Ibid., Section 4.5.1.2, p. 14.

7. *USMARC Format for Holdings and Locations*, draft 1/31/84 (Washington: Library of Congress, 1984), Foreword, F-2.

SISAC:
The Serials Industry Systems Advisory Committee

Minna C. Saxe

The purpose of this paper is to provide the reader with an overview of SISAC, the Serials Industry Systems Advisory Committee. This unique organization strives to facilitate the handling of serials by publishers, librarians, and users. Employing the diverse capabilities of automation for this purpose, SISAC has proceeded to develop and implement two important proposed voluntary serial standards.

BACKGROUND

Before discussing these standards, it is important to have some background information on the Committee. The Serials Industry Systems Advisory Committee was established in December 1982 as a committee of the Book Industry Study Group, Inc., a not-for-profit organization of book publishers, retailers, librarians, wholesalers, and manufacturers. (The Group had earlier established BISAC, the Book Industry Systems Advisory Committee, which had developed a voluntary standardized format for computer-to-computer ordering of monographs.) It was felt that such a format was also needed for serials and that this new format should be designed by those individuals who work with serials. In addition, it was noted that direction was needed for the development of both an

---

Minna C. Saxe is Chief Serials Librarian, City University of New York, Graduate School Library.

216 THE USMARC FORMAT FOR HOLDINGS AND LOCATIONS

issue-specific and article-specific code for serials. So it has been that SISAC, since its inception, has had as two primary goals: 1) to create a voluntary standardized format for the electronic transmission of serials data, and 2) to develop a standardized method to identify a serial issue as well as a specific article in a serial.

SISAC members, who include publishers, vendors, data-base producers, and librarians, have been working diligently to develop these formats and to promote their implementation. However, there is still a need for wider participation in SISAC, especially by librarians.[1]

SISAC, as a committee, meets bimonthly; four of these meetings take place in New York City and two meetings are held at the American Library Association Annual and Mid-Winter meetings. Each committee member also participates in the workings of one of SISAC's subcommittees. In this paper, the work of three of these subcommittees will be presented.

INTERNATIONAL STANDARD SERIAL NUMBER

As an aside (but a very important one), I must explain that it is my contention and has been for many years that almost all automation of serial activities has been possible only because there exists a standardized identification code for most serial titles. The International Standard Serial Number (ISSN) is the concise title identification code which appears on serials and also in bibliographic citations for these serials. Some librarians will immediately take exception to this statement and will argue that although the ISSN has been a standard for many years, a large number of publications do not use the code. In order to determine which statement is correct, I conducted a small survey of the periodical titles which are received by the library in which I work. During a 4-week period in September 1986, 88% of the issues sampled had ISSNs on them. Of course, many issues carried the code in a less than obvious location. Nevertheless, I consider this percentage most significant: the ISSN was used on an overwhelmingly large number of publications in our sampling. From our small survey it appears that publishers are indeed consistently providing serial title identification codes on their publications.

It is also most interesting to note that although 12% of the titles in our sampling had no ISSNs on them, 2% of the titles sampled did have the proposed code for issue-specific information. It is most significant as this new code is the product of the concerted effort of the members of SISAC Subcommittee 1.

THE SISAC BAR CODE

Subcommittee 1, chaired by Wendy Reidel of the Library of Congress, has developed the code for serial issue and article identifiers. This SISAC Subcommittee is now also the NISO(Z39) Standards Committee CC. (NISO is the abbreviation for the National Information Standards Organization and is the accredited developer of all standards concerning information science, publishing, and library science for the American National Standards Institute [ANSI]. ANSI, in turn, is the official U.S. member of the International Organization for Standardization [ISO].)

Part of SISAC Subcommittee 1's work is covered in the *NISO Draft Standard Z39.56-198x* which is the human-readable code for both serial issue and article identifiers. An example of this code is shown in Figure 1. It is evident that the code requires the eight-digit ISSN as its basis; the ISSN is transposed conventionally as four digits, a hyphen, four digits and serves, as always, as the unique title identifier. The next group of elements is the issue identification code and it consists of two parts: the chronology statement in parentheses followed by the enumeration statement (which can be expanded up to four levels, plus an additional level to indicate a supplement or index. The four levels in the enumeration are differentiated by colons, and a supplement is shown by a plus sign, " + ," an index by an asterisk, "*"). If only issue identification is

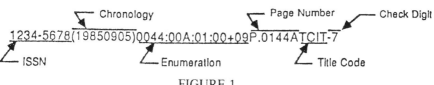

FIGURE 1

to be shown, the next and last element would be a check digit preceded by a hyphen, as shown in Figure 2.

When article information is to be shown, as in Figure 1, the data area will contain the initial page number of the article and, if more than one article *starts* on the same page, a title code, using "the first letter of each of the first four words of the title which contain four or more characters."[2] Please note that an important change has been proposed for this portion of the format. It has been recommended that there be a colon inserted between the last character of the page number and the first character of the title code. The article identification area would therefore read: "P.0144A:TCIT." The final element in Figure 1 is the check digit preceded by a hyphen. So, to review: the elements in the NISO draft standard consist of the ISSN (which is the title identifier), the chronology and enumeration (which comprise the issue identifier), the page number and title code (which comprise the article identifier), and the check digit.

SISAC Subcommittee 1 has also worked on the conversion of the issue identifier into a bar code or machine-readable format. Mr. George Wright, member of SISAC and the President of Periodical Identification & Processing Systems Inc., has recommended a new symbology, code 128, which he considers a most versatile symbology and most appropriate for SISAC's use. This symbology is shown in the bar code in Figure 2, above the human-readable code. This combination of the human-readable code and the bar code ap-

FIGURE 2

peared on 2% of the periodicals received at the library during the test described earlier.

Everyone is accustomed to seeing bar codes on a wide variety of items at grocery stores, as well as on mass circulation magazines and paperbacks. Many of these items use a symbology other than code 128, but, in all cases, these codes can be read by a variety of means, such as by light pen or by laser scanner.

It is very easy to anticipate the many uses librarians can make of the issue and article identification codes, in either a manual or an automated library environment. Indeed, after the issue identification code appeared on the June 1986 issue of *American Libraries*, Deas P. Campbell, a librarian at Texas Woman's University in Denton, wrote the following in a letter to the editor of *American Libraries*: "Barcoding serials just might be the best idea since library paste!"[3] Obviously, Deas Campbell can anticipate the various uses of the machine-readable code in library operations.

TESTING USE OF THE SISAC BAR CODE

In fact, a test of library use of the SISAC bar code has been completed for the period April through October 1986. Mary Ellen Clapper, chair of SISAC Subcommittee 5, has completed the coordination of the testing of the SISAC bar code in libraries, as well as an evaluation of the usability of the proposed serial issue identifier and bar code symbology by libraries, publishers, and vendors. For the participating libraries, a two-part evaluation form was designed: Part I of this form was completed each month by the individual who checked in the serials by using the machine-readable bar code. The questions asked in this part primarily concern the readability of the bar codes on the periodicals. Part II, which was completed at the end of the test period by each participating institution, asked for information on the library's overall impressions on using a bar code reading system, and for suggestions of other publishers who should be contacted by SISAC to use bar codes on their publications (Figures 3 and 4).

The results of these library evaluations indicate that the test libraries were most enthusiastic about the checking in of serials by using the machine-readable bar codes. Two important factors, accu-

220 THE USMARC FORMAT FOR HOLDINGS AND LOCATIONS

JULY 1986

SISAC LIBRARY EVALUATION FORM: PART I

SISAC TEST

Please fill out 1 form per person per month.

1. Name:_____ Month: _____ Year: _____

2. Institution: _____

3. Online serials control system used: _____

4. Bar code reading system used: _____

5. Estimated total number of issues checked in monthly: _____

6. Number of *issues* checked in using the bar code reading system: _____

7. Number of *titles* checked in using the bar code reading system: _____

8. Number of issues having bar codes which you were unable to check-in
using the bar code reading system: _____

Please specify why the bar code was unreadable:

9. Was it covered with a mailing label? ☐ Yes ☐ No

10. Was it damaged or mutilated in some other way? ☐ Yes ☐ No

If yes, please explain: _____

11. Was there insufficient differentiation between bar code and paper coloration? ☐ Yes ☐ No

12. Was the serials control system bar code reading system inoperable? ☐ Yes ☐ No

13. Any other reasons? Please explain: _____

14. Did you save time by using the bar code reading system? ☐ Yes ☐ No

Please explain: _____

15. How often was it necessary to do multiple reads?
☐ Always   ☐ Most times   ☐ Sometimes   ☐ Seldom   ☐ Never

Please explain: _____

16. How often was it necessary to enter the human readable string?
☐ Always   ☐ Most times   ☐ Sometimes   ☐ Seldom   ☐ Never

Please explain: _____

17. Did the *location* of the bar code on the issue have any effect on using the
bar code reading system? ☐ Yes ☐ No

Please explain: _____

THANK YOU!

FIGURE 3

Minna C. Saxe 221

JULY 1986

SISAC LIBRARY EVALUATION FORM: PART II

SISAC TEST

Please fill out 1 form per institution.

1. Name: _____ Period covered: _____

2. Institution: _____

3. Online serials control system used: _____

4. Bar code reading system used: _____

5. Estimated number of periodical titles currently received: _____

6. Number of periodical titles checked in using the bar code reading system: _____

7. Please list other periodicals you would like to see adopt the SISAC code: _____
_____
_____

8. Please list other publishers you would like to see adopt the SISAC code: _____
_____
_____

9. Please list other vendors you would like to see adopt the SISAC code: _____
_____
_____

10. Would you be willing to contact the companies you have listed above and
recommend that they use the SISAC code? ☐ Yes ☐ No

Please explain: _____
_____

11. What is your institution's overall impression of using a bar code reading system
with the SISAC code? (For example, does it add to the efficiency of your operation?
For what other purposes could it be used?) _____
_____
_____

12. Please use the reverse side for additional comments.

THANK YOU!

FIGURE 4

222 THE USMARC FORMAT FOR HOLDINGS AND LOCATIONS

racy and speed, were also noted earlier in the article in *SISAC News* as advantages of using machine-readable data rather than keyboarding data:

> If you want to give a computer information, why not just use a keyboard to type it in? [However,] even the best typists make about one error every 300 keystrokes. That type of error is called a substitution error — one in which the wrong character gets substituted for the correct one. In contrast to keyboard entry, . . . bar code systems are . . . more accurate. They make one substitution error every 15,000-100,000,000 characters. . . . As you can see, [the] bar code format . . . [is] much less error prone than even the best typists. . . . [Reading a bar code is] also very fast. . . . Bar code data entry is about twenty times faster than a keyboard![4]

As to the mechanics of bar code reading, there were several specific comments, such as that a bar code cannot be read if a mailing label has been placed over it. (Unfortunately, this did occur and, of course, made the reading impossible.) The participants indicated no preference as to where the bar code should be placed on the journals; although most journals had the bar code on the front cover, several journals used the back cover for this purpose. Test libraries indicated that both locations were acceptable. The use of a laser scanner to read the bar code was found to be more efficient than a light pen, which was more prone to mechanical difficulties.

The overall impressions by the test libraries indicate that they foresee a definite use for this procedure as the number of journals with the SISAC bar code increases. From the library's perspective, it is only time and cost effective to use bar code reading equipment for check-in if there is a sufficiently large number of journals which use the code. In addition, it was hoped that the vendors of the automated serials control systems would enhance their systems so that the bar code reading would not only access the online information but would also check in the issue. The libraries anticipate many uses of the serial issue and article identifiers (both in human-readable as well as machine-readable formats) for ordering and for citing in interlibrary loan, indexing, and abstracting.

For the test period, 22 publishers had agreed to use bar codes on a selected number of their publications. In most cases, these publishers were learned societies, university presses, and, in general, representatives of scholarly and professional serial publications. This type of publisher reflected SISAC's priority, at that time, to concentrate on the nonmass-circulation sector of serial publishing.

The participating publishers were also requested to complete evaluation forms at the end of the test period. The publishers, in general, experienced no problem in the printing of bar codes on their publications, although it was noted that in two cases unsuitable background color interfered with the reading of the bar code.

An important matter for the publishers concerned the physical location of the bar code on the journal; the front cover locations, which had been prescribed by SISAC, were not always found to be acceptable. Alternative locations, as options, were asked for by the publishers; these locations include the back cover, the inside cover, or the copyright page.

Some publishers did express concern about such matters as the costs of providing bar codes on their publications as well as the production delays that such a new procedure generated. The publishers were about evenly split on the issue of producing bar codes in-house or obtaining them from a vendor.

As to future applications of bar coding, publishers anticipated its use within their operations for subscription fulfillment, inventory control, and returns. There was also a general consensus that broader publisher participation would be dependent upon the clear demonstration of benefits to them and the strong indication by libraries that the use of bar codes was necessary for their operations.

Several library system vendors were queried as to the implementation process needed to enhance their systems to read the SISAC bar code for the serial check-in process. As all the systems used the ISSN as a search key, it was simply a matter of parsing and storing the other elements of the SISAC code; this is what most vendors did or plan to do. The vendors did agree that the cost and time involved in terms of implementation was not prohibitive and that the implementation was worth the investment.

The vendors' prognoses were dependent upon more publishers using the SISAC code. Vendors saw both the long-term benefits for

224 THE USMARC FORMAT FOR HOLDINGS AND LOCATIONS

libraries as well as the enhanced value of their own automated systems from the use of the code, but they concurred that neither was probable unless many more serials had the SISAC code on them.

A more detailed analysis of the evaluations by libraries, publishers, and system vendors, as well as background information on the test, are found in the document "The SISAC Test Report," dated January 16, 1986, compiled by Mary Ellen Clapper, which appears in the February 1987 issue of *SISAC News*. This document also contains samples of all the evaluation forms and a listing of participants.

ELECTRONIC TRANSMISSION OF SERIALS DATA

SISAC's second goal, to create a voluntary standardized format for the electronic transmission of serials data has been the work of SISAC Subcommittee 2, chaired by Asha Capoor of Baker & Taylor. Subcommittee 2 has also become NISO(Z39) Standards Committee DD, and it has produced the *NISO Draft Standard Z39.55-198x* on computerized serials orders, claims, cancellations, and acknowledgments. Based upon both the BISAC and MARC formats, this proposed standard, called SOCCA by some, is "intended to be a carrier format for exchange structure of the data within individual systems."[5] The standard states that each electronically transmitted record consist of a leader, a directory, the data, and a record terminator. (These are all familiar terms to librarians using the MARC formats.) The data fields and the subfields are of variable length and cover such categories as control number, business arrangements, vendor and customer information, and line items.

When using this draft standard, it is possible to transmit data in any one of three levels of complexity; level 1, the minimum level for a record, consists only of the ISSN or the International Standard Book Number (ISBN), the Standard Address Number (SAN), and the serial issue and/or article identifier; the draft reads that "titles, addresses, etc. are not expressed, except by ISBN, ISSN, serial issue/article identifier or SAN."[6] In other words, only codes are used. It is suggested that level 1 be used for renewals or for ordering items with ISBNs or serial issue or article identifier. On the other hand, level 2 records contain, in addition to the information included in level 1, amplification of the vendor or customer ship-to and bill-to data. Level 3 records expand line item information, in addition to including any elements of level 1 or level 2. The levels of complexity are coded in leader position no. 7, with level 1 coded as "A," level 2 as "B," and level 3 as "C."

Another very important part of the leader is position no. 5, where the required status code must be indicated: "A" for acknowledgment, "C" for claims, "D" for cancel, "R" for renewal, etc. Members of SISAC Subcommittee 2 have also complied an excellent 14-page data dictionary, which serves both as a dictionary and as an index to the data elements.

Both draft standards were circulated to the voting members of NISO(Z39) and other interested parties in early 1986. The NISO office has received many comments and has forwarded them to the two chairpersons. Since Spring 1986, both Subcommittees 1 and 2 have held meetings to discuss the comments.

CHANGES IN THE SISAC CODE

The primary criticism of Subcommittee 1's work has been the dependence of the code on the ISSN, as the issue and article identifiers cannot be constructed for journals which do not have ISSNs. There also have been comments questioning the limitation of the enumeration statement to four levels as there exist periodicals with five or more levels of enumeration. SISAC has recommended that the Introduction to the *NISO Draft Standard Z39.56-198x* emphasize that this standard is intended to cover approximately 80% of all serials, which has always been the intent of SISAC. Although some NISO(Z39) standards cover every item in their universe, others are more restrictive, and this standard falls into the latter category.

As of January 1987, Subcommittee 1 is in the process of incorporating several proposal changes into its draft standard. For the most part, these changes are editorial in nature, except for the use of the colon which is to be inserted between the page number and the title code as discussed earlier. In addition, the revised draft will include a great number of examples, many of which were provided by Subcommittee member Ron Gardner of OCLC, Inc. With the completion of an expanded and revised Introduction, which will clarify in detail the major criticisms concerning the dependence on the ISSN to construct the proposed code and the 80% coverage application, Subcommittee 1 intends to send a revised draft standard to NISO by Spring 1987. The revised draft will then be subject to the NISO member vote.

The comments received by Subcommittee 2 have been incorporated into a revised draft, dated October 1986; in addition, the Subcommittee has included with the document a six page listing of the changes. Subcommittee members are also writing prefatory essays which will provide information on the scope of the standard and will suggest guidelines and samples for the proposed standard's use. The revised draft standard was made available for comments and will be sent to the NISO office to be distributed to voting members.

CONCLUSION

The SISAC membership can rightfully be proud of its accomplishments to date. In large part this is due to the excellent leadership which SISAC had and currently has: Richard Rowe of The Faxon Company served as Chair of SISAC from its beginnings to 1986 and has been succeeded by Mary E. Curtis of Transaction Publishers. Sandra Paul of SKP Associates has served as the Book Industry Study Group Managing Agent. In addition to the three subcommittee chairpersons whose committees' activities have been presented, Patricia Sabosik, editor and publisher of *Choice*, has served as chair of the Membership and Publicity Subcommittee, as well as editor of *SISAC News*.

In addition, SISAC has maintained a close and supportive relationship with the National Information Standards Organization (NISO), as witnessed by two SISAC subcommittees also being NISO (Z39) standard committees. Patricia Harris, executive director of NISO, has been most helpful in maintaining these ties.

SISAC's future activities will include an active campaign publicizing the need to use the SISAC code on a large number of serials. One important task for librarians will be contacting publishers to use the code; all librarians interested in expediting the processing of serials should participate. Joining and promoting SISAC is important for all librarians, publishers, and vendors.

NOTES

1. For more information on SISAC, please contact Bill Raggio at SISAC, 160 Fifth Avenue, New York, NY 10010.

2. National Information Standards Organization, *Draft Z39.56-198x* (February 1986): 7.

3. *American Libraries* 17, no. 7 (July/August 1986): 510.

4. *SISAC News* 1, no. 1 (October 1985): 10.

5. Serials Industry Systems Advisory Committee, *Draft Proposal for National Information Standards Organization Draft Z39.55-198x* (October 1986): 1.

6. Ibid.: 4.

Index

AACR2 11,191,195,197
American National Standard for Information Science-Serial Holdings Statements (ANSI Z39.44-1986) 4, 8,10,14,15,24,25,32,35,55,56,74, 75,76,84,90,115,142,146,147,168, 170,188,191,194,197,201,207,209, 212
American National Standard for Serial Holdings Statements at the Summary Level (ANSI Z39.42-1980) 4,13,14, 62,146,193,199,200,201,204
American National Standard for Holdings Statements for Non-Serial Items (Z39.57) 74,188,193

Bar Code Symbology 95,218
BISAC 215,224
Boston Library Consortium 157,160
Boston University 160
Brodart 153,156

Carlyle 153,160
Chronology 4,5,10,11,14,15,20-34,55,56, 74,85,95,106,111,112,115,117,142, 145,147,148,168,171,189,192,198, 201,204,205,217,218
COM 57,104
CODEN 12,17,197
CONSER 51,62,137,141,170,193
Council on Library Resources 193

Data Compression 27-28,40,53-55,63,65, 75-76,94,110,111,114,127-128,156, 161,163,164,165,166,167,168, 170-171,189,207-208
Data Expansion 28-29,65,75-76,110,111, 163,169,189
DRA 160
Dynix 160

Emory University 1,6,138
Enumeration 4,5,10,11,14,15,20-34,55,56, 74,75,76,85,95,106,109,111,112, 115,129,142,145,147,148,168,171, 189,192,198,201,204,205,217,218, 225

FAXON Company 91,143-172
Florida Center for Library Automation 141
Florida State University 1
Florida Union List of Serials 137

GEAC 153,160

Harvard University 40,61-77
HOLLIS 61,63,64,65,68,69,70,71,77

Indexes 33-34,127,168,205-207
INNOVACQ 100
International Standard for Bibliographic Description 195
ISBN 12,165,224
ISSN 12,17,95,148,197,216-217,224,225

LAMBDA 41,42,43,45,46,138,141,142
LCCN 12,17
Library of Congress 6,7,35,40,51,62,123, 137,141,170
LIAS (Pennsylvania State University) 153
LINX 144,167
LS/2000 153,160
LUIS (NOTIS) 178-179

MARC 4,6,7,13,15,34,37,43,46,48,51,53, 56,57,62,63,64,65,66,70,71,74,82, 90,105,124,126,128,145,147,151, 156,1,74,180,191
MARC field tags.
   001 12
   004 12

© 1988 by The Haworth Press, Inc. All rights reserved.

007 10,11,16,154,181,182,183,188
008 11,16,44,46,48,51,154,181,182,
    183,188
010 12
014 12,17,154,164
020 12
022 12
023 12
024 12
027 12
030 12
035 12,17,140
098 44
099 19,44
245 43
590 46,48
846 186
85X 45,50,52,108,114
852 17,18,19,20,34,44,46,47,48,49,51,
    57,66,69,73,90,107,108,114,117,
    118,119,125,127,154,155,161,183,
    184,185,186
853 20,21,22,23,24,25,26,27,28,29,30,
    32,33,34,35,48,49,50,53,54,55,66,
    68,69,71,75,76,84,85,86,87,88,90,
    94,96,106,107,108,109,110,111,
    112,113,114,115,117,118,119,125,
    127,130,138,147,148,155,160,161,
    162,163,164,170,171,189
854 21,32,33,34,50,54,75,111,112,113,
    114,117,125,127,129,189
855 21,33,34,50,54,93,111,112,113,
    114,117,125,127,189
86X 45,51,52,53,54,108,111,129
863 19,20,21,22,23,24,25,26,27,28,29,
    30,31,32,33,34,35,44,48,51,52,54,
    66,68,69,71,73,74,75,76,85,86,87,
    88,90,94,95,96,106,108,109,111,
    113,114,115,117,118,119,125,127,
    130,148,155,160,161,162,163,164,
    165,166,189
864 21,33,34,51,52,54,73,85,114,117,
    125,127,129,155,166,189
865 21,33,34,51,52,54,73,85,93,114,
    117,125,127,166,189
866 26,34,35,48,51,53,68,69,71,73,75,
    85,86,88,106,125,127,146,155,156,
    160,161,162,163,164,166,167,189,
    190

867 34,73,85,93,127,189,190
868 34,73,85,127,185,189,190
MARBI Committee 7,36,43,73,167
MARVEL (University of Georgia) 80,81,
    82,84,85,87,90,91,94,95,162,
    163-164
Massachusetts Institute of Technology 160
MicroLINX 91,94,95,143,145,147,148,
    156,160,162-167

National Information Standards
    Organization 3,4,39,40,42,55,56,
    57,173,174,226
NOTIS 64,68,69,70,138,140,167,173-190
Northwestern University Library 176

OCLC 4,13,17,19,48,51,52,80,104,137,
    142,226
OCLC MARC field tags
    049 19,45,46,48,51
    910 46,48
    949 46,48

Pennsylvania State Universtiy 153
Publication Pattern 10,11,20-34,50,54,65,
    73,75,82,84,85,86,87,94,96,110,
    111,114,117,130,133,138,140,145,
    147,163-164,167,169,170,171

Research Libraries Groups 17,62
Research Libraries Information Network
    17,62

SAN 224
SC-10 144,145,146,147,151-159,160,161,
    162,167
SISAC 95,215-227
SISAC Bar Code 95,148,149,217-224
Southeastern Library Network (SOLINET)
    35,39-59
Southeastern Association of Research
    Libraries (SEARL) 1,5,39,40,41,
    46,50,51,55,57,73,138
Southeastern Association of Research
    Libraries (SEARL) Cooperative
    Serials Project 6,35,39,193
Sperry 153
Supplements/Accompanying Materials
    32-33,127,168,205-207

Index

Union List 4,13,15,34,57,64,65,67,68,126, 190,211
Union List (FAXON) 143,144,145,146, 152,157-162
University of Florida 1,6,137-142
University of Georgia 6,40,79-97,162
University of Kentucky 1,138
University of Miami (Florida) 1
University of Tennessee 1

University of Wyoming 153,156
USMARC 4,16,63,64,65,68,70,102,116, 174
USMARC Advisory Group 7,35

Virginia Polytechnic Institute and State University 1,6,123
VTLS 123-135,153,167

WLN 41